A. E. HOUSMAN

Poetry and Prose: A Selection

HUTCHINSON ENGLISH TEXTS

A. E. HOUSMAN

Poetry and Prose: A Selection

Edited by

F. C. HORWOOD

HUTCHINSON EDUCATIONAL

HUTCHINSON EDUCATIONAL LTD
3 Fitzroy Square, London W1

London Melbourne Sydney Auckland
Wellington Johannesburg Cape Town
and agencies throughout the world

First published October 1971
Reprinted October 1972

THE COLLECTED POEMS OF A. E. HOUSMAN
is published by Jonathan Cape Limited
by arrangement with whom this
edition is published

Poems: Copyright by the Estate of A. E. Housman
Extracts from *Introductory Lecture, Books I and V of Manilius* and *The Name*
and Nature of Poetry reproduced by permission of the Cambridge
University Press
© this edition F. C. Horwood 1971

This book has been set in Spectrum type, printed in Great Britain
on smooth wove paper by Anchor Press, and
bound by Wm. Brendon, both of Tiptree, Essex

ISBN 0 09 108770 8 (cased)
0 09 108771 6 (paper)

Contents

Introduction

Two volumes of Housman's poetry, containing 104 poems, were published in his lifetime under his own supervision, plus some lines acting as prelude to *Last Poems*. After his death another 71, *not selected by him*, were published by his brother Laurence, together with some verses acting as prelude to *More Poems*. The *Collected Poems* (Jonathan Cape) add 23 more selected by Laurence (*Additional Poems*), plus three translations, all early, and all previously published, from Greek tragic dramatists. The present selection consists of 100 poems. There are many chips from Housman's workshop in his four notebooks, dismembered by Laurence, and these throw great light on his methods of composition.

A Shropshire Lad made its way slowly. Housman, like Wordsworth, wished to be a popular poet, and paid for the publication himself. The boom in his poetry came with the First World War, perhaps helped by the impact of *Epitaph on an Army of Mercenaries*, which was published in *The Times* of 31 October 1917. Housman had already been asked by Professor Sir Walter Raleigh, for whom he made an exception in his contempt for academic critics, whose approval he thought 'the second death', for permission to include some of his lyrics in an anthology for soldiers in September 1915. A collection of his poems (all but five) was made for American Armed Forces early in the Second World War. Housman has never been out of print since *A Shropshire Lad* appeared in 1896. The evidence shows that he has meant much to many, young and old, has expressed their hearts, and, paradoxically enough in view of some aspects of his message, consoled them.

In the 26 years which elapsed between 1896 and 1922, Housman learnt nothing and forgot nothing. It is impossible to tell from internal evidence what poems he wrote first and what last. It seems to be pure chance that his most beautiful poem, as many think, 'Tell me not here, it needs not saying' was written in 1922, when he was 62; in thought and workmanship it differs little from *The Merry Guide* of 1890. When *More Poems* was published in 1936, an Oxford professor (Garrod) especially praised for its maturity the last poem, *Parta Quies* (No. 99, see p. 179). This was written when Housman was an undergraduate of 20. The poems of *Last Poems* and *More Poems* were written at various, sometimes widely separated dates, but they show no sign of this that I can discern. Similarly, there appears to be no significant order in the poems published in Housman's lifetime: his only principle, if that, seems to have been one of contrast, except that in both volumes, naturally enough, the last poems are 'farewell' poems. In spite of what I have said, however, it may be of some *poetic* significance that composers, who have been attracted to Housman as bees to flowers, have overwhelmingly gone for *A Shropshire Lad*, and mainly neglected *Last Poems* and the rest.

The scene of Housman's poems, where they have one, is at least as much a country of the mind as of cartography. Or it is remembered country, 'the land of lost content', even the townsman's dream of the country, like most pastoral.[1] The sprinkling of Shropshire names is thickest in *A Shropshire Lad*, thin in *Last Poems*, and reduced to one (Wales) in *More Poems*. Names like Abdon Burf, Clee, Teme, Corve, Wenlock Edge, and so on, give a rural fragrance to the poems and a sense of locality which is part illusion. Housman was quite capable of putting Hughley and its steeple (No. 42) on a hill, instead of in its true location in a valley, and peopling the north side with suicides among nettles, instead, as Laurence pointed out, 'of the respectable churchwardens and wives of vicars, all in neatly tended graves'. Housman later said that the place he really meant had an ugly name.

But if precise locality was not a particular point with him, his natural world is singularly lovely. For 20 years he kept a diary of the first blossoming of trees and flowers. He said of Tennyson that he would be the one poet whom a blind lover of the countryside would wish to know by heart. He has the same accuracy as Tennyson, which is not plain transcription or catalogue, but a transmutation into imaginative phrase or line or epithet: the sheaves which 'stand still all night' and are 'marshalled under moons of harvest'; the beeches which 'strip in storms for winter'; the pine which 'lets fall its cone'; the lady-smocks that 'a-bleaching lay'; the bluebells that 'like a skylit water stood'. These and many others are felicities beyond the reach of the mere observer, however loving. The great poem 'Tell me not here' is a love-story, a hopeless passion for a most beautiful and seductive enchantress. Housman has none of Wordsworth's beliefs about the nature of Nature. He expressed what he thought about such fancies in *The Name and Nature of Poetry*: 'The

[1] Except that this townsman knew a good deal *exactly* about the country.

9

Wordsworthians', he says, '. . . accepted his belief in the morality of the universe and the tendency of events to good; they were even willing to entertain his conception of Nature as a living and sentient and benignant being, a conception as purely mythological as the Dryads and the Naiads'. Housman is so remote from this conception that he even takes care (when he remembers, and as far as it is possible for mind itself to do so[1]) to disassociate himself from the pathetic fallacy:[2]

> The sigh that heaves the grasses
>   Whence thou wilt never rise
> Is of the air that passes
>   And knows not if it sighs.
>
> The diamond tears adorning
>   Thy low mound on the lea,
> Those are the tears of morning,
>   That weeps, but not for thee. (No. 64)

He is equally remote from the 'Tennysonian' conception, the Nature of the evolutionists, red in tooth and claw, grand but not benignant. Nature in Shropshire and Worcestershire is not apt to impress one with its ferocity. In his most moving nature poem, Nature is 'heartless, witless nature', a beautiful but imbecile mistress; she smiles, but is indifferent. But how heartbreakingly lovely she is! He is far enough away from Wordsworth not to have his

---

[1] Of course, it is not quite possible for mind—at least, poetic mind—to do so, as we see from the poem quoted on p. 11.

[2] *pathetic fallacy*: a term invented by Ruskin (*Modern Painters*). He meant by it the habit of crediting Nature with human emotions, and, especially, the idea of Nature sympathising with human feelings.

consolations; but perhaps nor far enough not to regret them. And perhaps he has one of them, for he seems to believe, as Wordsworth did, that skies will knit men's heart-strings right, and fields will breed them brave (*ASL I*).[1] More than this, Nature is a friend, as mortal men are friends, for she too is doomed and makes the same journey. And at least she can *seem* to sympathise:

> The earth, because my heart was sore,
> Sorrowed for the son she bore;
> And standing hills, long to remain,
> Shared their short-lived comrade's pain.
> And bound for the same bourn as I,
> On every road I wandered by,
> Trod beside me, close and dear,
> The beautiful and death-struck year. (No. 31)

Housman greatly admired Horace (see No. 80, and note); and it has been said of Horace's poems that those most typical of his genius are those which contrast the beauty and permanence of nature with the shortness of man's life, like Odes I. 4 (*Solvitur acris hiems*) or IV. 7 (*Diffugere nives*). This contrast is certainly present in Housman, but permanence is not a possibility in him. Even 'the standing hills' only stay longer.

I should reckon Housman among the major nature poets, certainly in lyric shape, both in scope and expression. No Englishman who loves the shires and country-side can escape him; no one can fail to be excited by the beauty and exactness of phrase, the nostalgia and affection of sentiment with which he has expressed the external

[1] For abbreviations see p. 185.

world. No poet can more safely be depended upon to release modern man's dumb feeling in the country, and few can have expressed them with more distinction. The smaller 'goings-on', in Wordsworth's words, of nature are among his successes, but he has his grandeurs too, sometimes astronomical, as in *Revolution* (No. 71), or *Reveille* (No. 3), or the wider view from the headlands of England out to Wales with 'silent hills indenting/The orange band of eve' (No. 92), or, with a combination of the homely situation of man and his dramatic environment:

> I see the air benighted
>   And all the dusking dales,
> And lamps in England lighted,
>   And evening wrecked on Wales. (No. 92)

Some poems, like 'Loveliest of trees' (No. 1) seem given up to nature entirely, but time creeps in as a shadow; and the only poem entirely devoted to sheer unreflective enjoyment is the beautiful lyric (No. 82) which Laurence selected from the notebooks:

> When green buds hang in the elm like dust
>   And sprinkle the lime like rain,
> Forth I wander, forth I must,
>   And drink of life again.
> Forth I must by hedgerow bowers
>   To look at the leaves uncurled,
> And stand in fields where cuckoo-flowers
>   Are lying about the world.

This simple content, this unmixed pleasure, is more like W. H. Davies than anything else in Housman; and no doubt, if Housman had had a hand in its publication, some sort of reminder of the unappeasable lot of man, of some thorns among the hedgerow bowers, would have invaded the poem.

'Imaginary Shropshire', said J. P. Bishop, 'is a country that belongs to the dead.' If this were true we should have none of the frustration, the suicidal agony, the love-longing, the place-nostalgia, the high hopes and vexations of youth, the delight in tree, flower and land which animates the figures of Shropshire lads and girls and the poet speaking (stylistically, at least) in his own person. Housmanland does not belong to the dead but to the doomed; but then, so does the whole of nature. In the interim, however, men think, drink, suffer, work, fight, hope, seduce, or try to seduce, girls, commit suicide or murder, enlist, dance, enjoy and endure. 'Imaginary Shropshire' is all too much alive. Moreover, it is mainly a land of youth or of a man recalling youth, the time of hope, of love, of expectation, of uncommon sensibility, of eagerness and freshness. This does not mean that the feelings of his poems is in any way immature; it is merely acuter, more expectant, and so more baffled:

> May will be fine next year as like as not:
> Oh ay, but then we shall be twenty-four (No. 50)

and somewhere there are

> Shires where the girls are fonder,
> Towns where the pots hold more (No. 92).

By far the greater number of the poems are in Housman's own poetic voice or voices. His use of the convention of the country-boy (he preferred 'lad', which he used 94 times as against three times for 'boy') is reserved for dramatic, even for melodramatic, or more rustic situations.

He preferred the rural to the rustic, and there is evidence from the notebooks that he cut down or out the more realistic agricultural touches. 'Terence this is stupid stuff' (No. 43) is, in part, his most rustic poem; but it was more rustic in draft, with such details as

> All spick and span went I and Ned
> . . . blue breast knots, neck ties gay
> Clean shirts, new ties, as blue as day.

This is well enough for a Hardy novel, but a little of it goes a long way in lyric. Housman himself appears as Terence, a dismal poet, in No. 43, and as the flautist in No. 75. (Housman was saved from the folly of calling his first volume *Poems by Terence Hearsay* by his friend, the scholar A. W. Pollard. Its poems would have made their way under any title, but surely more slowly under this.)

'The Shropshire Lad', said Housman, 'is an imaginary figure, with something of my temperament and view of life. Very little in the book is biographical.' He and his mates are a convenient fiction. In part they belong to the tragic world of the ballad, and so provide striking situations and occasions, far stronger than personal experience could have supplied Housman with. This, I take it, is what Louis Kronenberger means or partly what he means when he said: 'Housman transforms a way of thinking about life into a way of experiencing it'. The 'I' of the poems is as likely to be fictive as not, as far as experience goes, whatever aspect of Housman's thought he may truly express. What Housman said in the prelude verses to *More Poems* is true enough—if not all the truth—namely that 'the narrow measure' of his poems

> spans
> Tears of eternity, and sorrow,
> Not mine, but man's.

Particular situations and temperament are raised to the level of the universal

Among the young men of the poems none is more prominent than the soldier, or would-be soldier, and what has been called the 'romance of enlistment' is, together with other less cheerful aspects of the soldier's lot, a major theme. There is a large number of poems (over 20) written in admiration of or sorrow for British soldiers. Two of his best patriotic poems,* *ASL* I and No. 2, open *A Shropshire Lad*. The fourth (No. 3) puts a doctrine of energy and action into military terms. *Last Poems* is even more martial: seven out of the first eight are soldierly, and over one-third are soldier poems in one way or another. This probably means that Housman reduced their number in selecting his poems for *A Shropshire Lad* and re-picked them for *Last Poems* —not that he had become more military in the meantime. Probably his greatest patriotic poem is that masterpiece of irony, *Epitaph on an Army of Mercenaries* (No. 72).

He regarded patriotism as a dangerous subject for poets and as the virtue which had inspired the least amount of good poetry because it so easily degenerates into vice. He probably meant by this that patriotic poetry is likely to lapse into jingoism and sabre-rattling, the trap of bad, and sometimes of good poets, like Tennyson. Housman is never guilty of this, though his poetry first came out in the 90's, a decade striking for its jingoism, whose street-ballads fell into the depths of sentimentality, sadism and nonsense. But he took patriotism seriously, and once harshly snubbed Frank Harris for confidently and confidentially supposing that he did not.

It has been said that 'Housman got rid of his own unhappiness by laying it on the backs of marching soldiers' (Ruth Bailey), as if Housman's sense of life could be put in a knapsack. It has also been claimed that 'the real field of action and the headquarters from which the bulletins of resistance and retreat were dispatched were in his own warring consciousness, where he himself may be observed in all the combatants. He is each in turn, and sometimes even his foes'. This is finely said, but in fact only applies importantly to one poem, *The Welsh Marches* (No. 19). Generally applied, it is to take images for the things imaged. It ignores the objective presence of the soldier, or would-be soldier, in Housman's thought. He had a real notion of the unostentatious heroic, the unpretentious, unmarked and unconscious bravery of the common man.

Furthermore, his restless sons of men feel the deadly romance of enlistment:

> Far the calling bugles hollo,
>   High the screaming fife replies,
> Gay the files of scarlet follow:
>   Woman bore me, I will rise. (No. 25)

The Deserter (No. 54) is not a deserter from the army, but from the bed of his girl. Who can doubt that Housman in his soldier poems was struck more by the mortal than the martial, by the association of the young, vital and handsome with death—

> Lovely lads and dead and rotten (No. 25)?

Some critics have expressed surprise that a poet of his temper should have so much martial imagery, and so many martial figures. Perhaps, in place of 'martial' I should say 'poems about soldiers'; for it can safely be said that most of them could scarcely be used for recruiting propaganda—

> A soldier of the Queen, my lad,
> A bullet through the bean, my lad—

is so much, though not all, of their purport. The fight against odds always moved him. It is the spirit of man that is his theme, girded for a battle he must lose: he straps on the sword that will not save.

Housman is an acknowledged master of the simple and of plain expression. Few have managed the monosyllable to such powerful effect: whole lines or even stanzas may consist of nothing else, with little but an occasional disyllable or trisyllable to vary the movement. The clear elements of his vocabulary make an immediate impact: all is concrete, nothing abstract. Four-syllable words are rare, five-syllable words rarer (only two, I think). This means that even for lyric, the high proportion of monosyllables in his work is unusual. He has, however, a reasonable liking for compound epithets, especially in *A Shropshire Lad*, and there particularly in *The Merry Guide*, an early poem of 1890. These are of considerable beauty: 'rainy-sounding' (leaves), the 'valley-guarded' (granges), the 'sunstruck' (vanes), the 'moon-eclipsing' (cone of night) and so on. Equally beautiful, possibly less striking since they fit into phrases like fingers into gloves, are single epithets, like the 'blank' moon, the 'starlit' fences, an 'angry' dust, the 'brisk' brew of ale. The verbs, the words of action, are no less impeccable: the steeple which 'sprinkles' the quarters of the hour, the belfries which 'tingle', the clock which 'collected' its strength, the trains that 'groan' all night on the rail. The notebooks give ample evidence of his fastidiousness about word and phrase, and the hard work he put in to ensure their rightness: the famous 'coloured' of 'coloured counties' (No. 15) was the sixth choice; 'tossed' (No. 56) was reached after eight rejections, and 'rive' (No. 35) after eight tries. Sometimes the original attempts are obviously inept, quite unlike the finished Housman as we read him in print. He made a distinction between poetry that 'came into his head', and poetry that had to be 'composed', but if this means what it seems to mean, namely that his best poetry was spontaneous, the notebooks contradict him on many, if not perhaps all, sides. His lyrics, beautiful as they are, do not sound like lark-song, though some have that art that sounds like artlessness. His most colloquial expressions are usually confined to speakers in character, like the lad in No. 38 who commits suicide for his girl, and says to her 'for you I stopped the clock'; but the same kind of thing can be found in a more elevated poem such as *The Oracles* (**LP XXV*), where the inquirer says to the priestess 'there's better booze than brine'. Such locutions are not to be confused with proverbial or semi-proverbial, or homely phrases like 'Clay lies still, but blood's a rover', which retain their primitive power in his poems. Some of this is parallelled in his prose: for example, when he says of a scholar that he produces 'bucketfuls of falsehood', or asserts that the influences of literature run off most men 'like water off a duck's back'. These interpolations have power to refresh.

One could, of course, go on writing verse in monosyllables till the cows come home or till the crack of doom, without producing the effect of Housman's poems. Simplicity is not, in itself, an artistic virtue, but a mere abstraction, whose use, as in the ballad, can be impressive, but which can be banal or namby-pamby, as in some of Wordsworth's more aggressive experiments. The secret of Housman's style lies in compression and in economy. J. B. Priestley found the Roman lurking behind all the *Last Poems*, by which he meant that these lyrics, for all their softness, had 'that touch of iron, that suggestion of the chisel' that we associate with classical form. Housman was a great master of understatement, which is itself a form of the simple, but not the simple simple, rather the complex simple. More is implied than meets the eye. Housman is no Swift, but he has some share in that gift of saying coolly what could have been said passionately. Still, one mustn't think of Housman as invariably hard in texture and thought, as the idea of classical form might mislead one to do; things like 'Far in a western brookland' (No. 37), with its delicate sigh, and many others, would contradict this.

Nor does simplicity of diction mean simplicity of construction or of thought. The epigrammatic requires cunning and extreme thrift. The athlete who died young is congratulated on not outliving his honours and not joining the ranks of

> Runners whom renown outran
> And the name died before the man. (No. 13)

Simplicity in itself can be a form of irony: the *Epitaph on an Army of Mercenaries* (No. 72) is a full-length example of this, an example of diminution with ironic effect. One of its most striking instances in a line is in *ASL LI*, where the marble statue in the Grecian gallery advises the young countryman to

> Stand, quit you like stone, be strong.

This is already ironic enough; but it doubles its force when it is seen as a perversion of St Paul's adjuration to the Corinthians (I *Cor.* 16.3): 'quit you like men, be strong'; and redoubles this with its final couplet:

> 'And I stept out in flesh and bone
> Manful like the man of stone.'

The cleverness of this is obvious; and Housman is by no means averse to wit, conceit, and perhaps even to pun. There is the case of Dick's overcoat (No. 61), and the lovely conceit of the lady-smocks in No. 31.

> 'Or littering far the fields of May
> Lady-smocks a-bleaching lay.'

Here the country-name of the flower, its washed-out, very pale lavender colour, and the habit of bleaching linen, now perhaps obsolete, on grass are joined so shortly in a couple of lines which are wittily exact and happily pleasing. Housman's mind was not simple, and he did not always employ the simple simply.

In certain quarters, I believe, it is, or was, fashionable to speak of Housman's versification as monotonous. It is difficult to conceive of the kind of ear that could think it so. It is true that he had a great fondness for quatrains, and 130 of his 177 poems are written in this pattern. In the two volumes published in his lifetime there are 39 different measures, 28 of which were used only once. But these statistics say nothing about the internal quality of his line and stanza. There is every reason to suppose from his practice and his theory that he had a masterly understanding of the artifice of versification, and knew that he had. He would have preferred to speak on this topic in place of the topic he chose, *The Name and Nature of Poetry*, for his lecture in 1933. But the subject is not suitable for a lecture, and he contented himself with giving a short list of the matters he would have dealt with. This list is itself exciting and suggestive, and worth many pages of discussion in most other writers on versification. Among other matters, he mentions 'the office of alliteration in verse, and how its definition must be narrowed if it is to be something which can perform that office, and not fail of its effect or actually defeat its purpose'. The note-books show how often his revisions of earlier lines make them alliterative, without making them stick out like sore thumbs. There is none of the nonsense which occasionally marks Spenser's practice, such as

O foolish faerie's son, what fury mad.

Housman had a delicate and tactful sense of alliteration: it would be too much to say that head-rhyme mattered as much to his poetry as end-rhyme, but it is certainly important. But perhaps his greatest gift is one not so easily analysable, but immediately felt: his control of the pace and variety of line and stanza, so that the norm is never lost and never monotonously present. He knew that variety is the life of metre. The note-books show that rhythms sometimes came into his head without words.

He was a master of the use of words, which, while not directly onomatopoeic, have the quality of suggesting the objects and actions they name; hence, a phonetic richness, perhaps surprising in a poet who deals mainly in shorter lines.

He said in *The Name and Nature of Poetry* that 'poetry is not the thing said, but a way of saying it', and that poetry is 'more physical than intellectual'. It has been pointed out by a music critic that this is a definition of music as much as of poetry. It is clear from the lecture that an essential of poetry for Housman is incantation. He speaks of Shakespeare's 'Take, O, take those lips away' as 'nonsense; but it is ravishing poetry'. Still, he does admit that incantation joined to thought, as in 'Fear no more the heat o' the sun' in *Cymbeline*, gives a higher pleasure, indeed the highest pleasure.

His own poetry, in fact, is loaded with meaning. It also gives delight of uncommon appeal. His lines sometimes read as if he were permuting or ringing the changes on the vowels:

On the idle hill of summer,
    Sleepy with the flow of streams,
Far I hear the steady drummer
    Drumming like a noise in dreams. (No. 25)

The man with so fine an ear for the music of words had
none for the music of notes. He once wrote in a letter that
'neither illustrators nor composers care twopence about
words, and generally do not understand them'. Listening
to settings of his own poems appeared to give him pain,
perhaps acute pain. But if he had no use for composers,
they had much for him. He is to them what Heine was to
German composers. More than fifty of his poems have
been set to music in more than a hundred songs. The
favourite is the poem which opens this Selection—'Love-
liest of trees'—which has ten settings; then, in descending
order, No. 10 'When I was young and twenty' (8), No. 15
Bredon Hill (7), and No. 26 'White in the moon the long
road lies' (6). These, together with No. 3, *Reveille*, and No. 39
'With rue my heart is laden', have also been the favourites
with the anthologists. The music critic Ernest Newman
wrote in a letter to *The Sunday Times* (29 October 1922):
'Nowhere is there verse more apt for music', and he went
on to say that all but half a dozen of the sixty-three lyrics
of *A Shropshire Lad* 'cried out for music'. 'Never before has
an English poet produced so many poems having all the
requisites of poetry that is to be set to music: concision
and intensity of tone, the utmost simplicity of language,
freedom both from involution of structure and from
simile, and a general build that was virtually of musical
form. . . . Almost any one of these poems gave the com-
poser a central mood that was as truly musical as poetical,

while the vicissitudes of the poetic mood also suggested the natural stages of a musical idea.' This may not be all that is to be said about the formal beauty of the Housman lyric, but it is plenty. Newman does not find the same opportunities for the composer in *Last Poems*, and says that 'hardly more than half a dozen are first rate material for setting'. This may be because *A Shropshire Lad* represents Housman's first pick for publication. At all events, the taste of the composer and the reader do not coincide in this respect.

Housman said he was conscious of only three influences upon his poetry—the songs of Shakespeare, the Border Ballads, and Heine. He forgot to mention the Bible which was undoubtedly the greatest literary influence on him. A recent critic has listed over fourteen pages of parallels (not always important) of one sort or another between his poems and the Authorised Version—phrases, lines, half-lines, words and echoes, used with the ease and significance of long familiarity, so that they become an indistinguishable part of his style. Some are easily recognisable, some not, some so much a part of our language that they pass unnoticed as allusion. Job's reference to the dead 'that dwell in the houses of clay' is said of Fred—'clay's the house he keeps' (**ASL XXV*). 'All my bones shall say' of Psalm 35 becomes 'I hear my bones within me say' (No. 33); 'A dead man out of mind' (Ps. 31:12) is 'A dead man out of mind' of No. 44. It would be tedious to multiply examples of what is so frequent. Sometimes there is a conflation of more than one recollection. It would be easy to show, as indeed the few examples above do, that a prime source of the simple and unaffected strength of his writing is the Bible.

This constant reminiscence is not true of the ballad,

which can scarcely be traced in the same way in phrase and word,[1] though they also provide examples that show that some of the finest effects of art can be achieved by means of the simple. It is situation and manner, rather than phrase and word, which attracted him in the ballad, above all the tragic and doomed sense, the *lacrimae rerum* of the world. Few poets, if any, have better caught the manner of the traditional ballad, which often at its best is a core of dramatic situation, in monologue or dialogue. 'Is my team ploughing?' (No. 18) invites comparison with *The Wife of Usher's Well*, with its uncanny atmosphere, its spare drama, and its dialogue. In Keats's *La Belle Dame* there is a supernatural which is conscious of its own mystery: but the supernatural is taken for granted in Housman's poem, just as it is in the traditional ballad. 'Farewell to barn and stack and tree' (No. 6) seems to have behind it such a ballad as *Edward, Edward*.

As for Heine, both he and Housman shared a fondness for the measure, manner and stanza of the Volkslied, for the line of three or four accented syllables, for a basis, at least, of popular poetry, which extended even to colloquialisms, for which both have been criticised. Both are witty, both bitter, both nostalgic. Heine has been called the greatest exponent of romantic irony, and that seems to me to consist of placing the acid to the dream, to dream but always to wake up, as Heine does in *Aus alten Märchen winkt es*, or give a twist to his thought as he does in *Ich hab' im Traum geweinet*. But Housman, ironic as he is, does not sneer, as Heine can do. I find few specific relationships between them; but what has been called the distinctive feature of Heine's lyric, its 'arrested effusion', seems to me

[1] Partly because the simple is difficult to trace, except in phrase.

also characteristic of Housman. I should describe it as the firm artistic control over a flow or excess of emotion.

It is not the purpose of this Introduction to attempt any thorough investigation of what might be called the 'sources' of Housman's style and thought. Many years ago Professor George Gordon said in a lecture that 'the inquiry into sources is like going round to the back of a great man's house to see what parcels he receives'. Housman received many parcels from many sources. The style of classical poets, whom he knew so well, could obviously have little or nothing to say to the mechanics of English lyric but could teach economy and clarity. Housman did not think he was a classical poet, and placed classical poetry among unconscious influences upon him. If it is said that he learnt a philosophy from Lucretius, one could answer by saying that he could have found much the same thing in *Ecclesiastes*, or Greek tragedy, or Horace's Ode, *Diffugere Nives* (No. 80) or the great recitative of Empedocles, 'The out-spread world to span', from Arnold's *Empedocles on Etna*. He once, perhaps rashly, told a friend that this passage 'contained all the law and the prophets'; and it is clear that its determination to see the worst and make the best of things, its combination of clear-sightedness and courage, and such sentiments as

'To tunes we did not call our being must keep chime'

were congenial to him. The style as well as the thought of Arnold's *The Last Word* seems to have influenced him.

It is true that Lucretius's anti-religion goes beyond any of these, and conforms in its pagan way with Housman's curious view, reported by his brother, that Christianity was most harmful in its social application. This would agree with Lucretius's line

Tantum religio potuit suadere malorum
—How many evils could religion bring men to commit.
(*De Rerum Natura*, I, 101)

Lucretius made this comment on the sacrifice of Iphigenia by her father in order to secure a favourable wind, and speaks with disgust, which he makes us share, of the cruelty of what he calls 'religion'.

In general, Housman was attracted to poems, particularly lyric poems, which shared his temper, sad or melancholy or bitter, or delighted with the transient show of the outer world of nature. He found his affinities in the pagan world of the tragic ballad, in Lucretius, in *Ecclesiastes*, in Arnold, in Horace's 7th Ode of the IVth Book, above all in Shakespeare's 'Fear no more the heat o' the sun'. He felt strongly the sense of life expressed in Virgil's well-known line:

Sunt lacrimae rerum et mentem mortalia tangunt
—Here are the tears of things and mortal matters touch the heart. (*Aeneid*, I, 461)

Formally, he is as much in touch with Watts and Blake as any among the English lyrists. He thought Watts's simplicity superior to Pope's art, and says of his *Cradle Hymn*:

> Soft and easy is thy Cradle,
>   Coarse and hard thy Saviour lay,
> When his Birth-Place was a Stable
> And his softest Bed was Hay

—'This simple verse, bad rhyme and all, is poetry beyond Pope's'. We need not comment on the injustice to Pope, who has his own place, propriety and significance, outside Housman's purview. As for Blake, whom he thought the supreme, but meaningless lyrist, no one could be further, except formally, from his own work; for some of Blake's loveliest lyrics, including those Housman quotes, are private and need interrogation; none of Housman's do.

Housman called himself a Cyrenaic, and thus linked himself to a philosophy whose extremest and most logical adherent, Hegesias, the 'persuader to die', as he was called, denied the possibility of real pleasure, and advocated suicide as ensuring at least absence of pain. Cyrenaicism is the purest hedonism in the history of thought: pleasure is the only good. But since observation and experience show us that there is more pain than pleasure in the world, and unalloyed happiness is not to be found, all hedonism tends towards pessimism. Actually, Housman claimed that he was not a pessimist but a pejorist, one who believed that the world could be a worse place. To the simple man, this will often seem a distinction without much difference. Perhaps the fullest poetic statement of Housman's philosophy is to be found in 'Terence, this is stupid stuff' (No. 43), a piece with some of the rather grim humour that sometimes crops up in the poems, and great fortitude. He confesses in another poem (No. 100) that though the stars have not dealt him the worst they could do, that his pleasures are plenty, yet two major troubles reave him of rest:

'The brains in my head and the heart in my breast.'

The conditions for ease in this world are

'flint in the bosom and guts in the head'.

The message of one of his favourite poets, Lucretius, is that 'self . . . is the secret malady of each of us—for ever unsatisfied, for ever ill at ease; and death alone can free us from this foe that is of our own household' (quoted from W. H. Mallock's Preface to his translations from *Lucretius on Life and Death*). Much the same view is to be found in the great chorus from the *Oedipus Coloneus* of Sophocles (p. 181) that he chose to translate in 1890. His favourite books of the Bible were *Ecclesiastes* and *Job*, and to a lesser extent *Ecclesiasticus*. *Ecclesiastes* with its melancholy and noble beauty, its 'thorough-going discontent, which is at bottom religious, with all things temporal', its agnosticism about the fate of the soul after death, its belief that wisdom and virtue are not rewarded, impressed itself deeply upon him. It was a passage from this book (XI. 7–XII. 7) that he chose for his funeral service. This passage contains words which could almost be seen as a summary of his own outlook:

'Truly the light is sweet, and a pleasant thing it is for the eyes to behold the sun: but if a man live many years, and rejoice in them all; yet let him remember the days of darkness; for they shall be many. All that cometh is vanity.'

It is not to be expected that such an outlook had anything to do with Christianity. He claimed to have been a deist at 13, an atheist at 21. He thought in later life that it was a perusal of Lemprière's *Classical Dictionary* at the age of eight which first attached his affections to paganism: at any rate, the mind later followed the heart in this respect. He remained an atheist throughout his life; and his last poem, For My Funeral (No. 98), written in 1925, is, according to his brother, and indeed its own evidence, devoid of any belief in a conscious future life. The only poem which might be Christian, but which, in fact, is merely a suspended judgement, which threatens at any moment to come down on the other side, is the Easter Hymn (No. 76). His views of the failure of Christ's life is expressed in The Carpenter's Son (No. 34), a daring relocalisation and resetting of the Crucifixion in the general atmosphere of A Shropshire Lad.

It has been said that his bitterness at death and oblivion is natural to one whose anger is because Christianity ought to be true. Lucretius preached a 'gospel of a redemption not from the grave, but in it' (Mallock, op. cit.). If, Lucretius argued, there is no after-life, death has lost its terrors:

> Nil igitur mors est ad nos neque pertinet hilum,
> Quandoquidem natura animi mortalis habetur.

—Death, therefore, is nothing, and nothing to do with us, since the nature of the mind is mortal.

(De Rerum Natura, Book iii, 830–1)

And if, says Lucretius, we ask what of our pleasant home, our well-loved wife, and our tender little ones, the answer is that the dead know nothing of this. That Housman shared this philosophy to some extent is obvious, but he did not think the peace of the grave was a sufficient answer to the pains of life. Since life appears to have no ultimate meaning (and the individual personality no destiny), he speaks of it as a 'long fool's errand to the grave'. There is a fine passage in the *Introductory Lecture* (Appendix II, 1(b)) where Housman says that 'the light shed on the origin and destiny of man by the pursuit of truth in some directions is not altogether a cheerful light'. This is the voice, or, at least, one of the voices, of his day. In a book called *The Foundations of Belief*, Lord (then Mr) Balfour, in analysing the implications of scientific materialism, summed up the position of man in his world as it seems to have appeared to Housman, and many like him (though not to Balfour himself):

'Man, as far as natural science by itself is able to teach us, is no longer the final cause of the universe, the heaven-descended heir of all the ages. His very existence is an accident, his story a brief and transitory episode in the life of one of the meanest of the planets.'

And in another place:

'Man will go down to the pit, and all his thoughts will perish. The uneasy consciousness, which, in this obscure corner, has, for a brief space, broken the contented silence of the universe, will be at rest. Matter will know itself no longer, "Imperishable monuments" and "immortal deeds", death itself, and love stronger than death, will be as though they had never been. Nor will anything that *is* be better or worse for all that the labour, genius, devotion and suffering of man have striven through countless generations to effect.'

These words, some of the sourest and most impressive

ever written, were published in 1895, on the eve of the publication of *A Shropshire Lad*. In No. 97 Housman also expresses with reticent grandeur and profound melancholy the futility of all human endeavour, even the effort of art.

In spite of all this, he has been called a Christian. This is absurd on the face of it; but one can see in some poems, notably in the moving poem 'When Israel out of Egypt came' (No. 77), a longing to have been the recipient of a revelation and a faith that other men have:

> The heart goes where no footstep may
> Into the promised land.

Perhaps in a paradoxical sense one can say that Housman's anti-religion is itself religious. Perhaps this is what the selectors of poems for *The Penguin Book of Religious Verse* felt when they culled two of his poems, 'On Wenlock Edge' (No. 22), and 'Be still, my soul' (No. 35), even if one wonders at their choice.

Anyway, there is no Christian hope in Housman. He is a pagan who looks hungrily at the Christian world, but refuses its food. Like Hardy, he is determined to put the bitter asp of truth to the breast—

> . . . if way to the Better there be, it exacts a full
> look at the Worst (Hardy, *In Tenebris*)

He is even closer to Clough's

> Let fact be fact, and life the thing it can,
> And play no tricks upon my soul, O man.

(See No. 81—'I to my perils/Of cheat and charmer'.)

Are then his poems an unrelieved sigh for what, in the nature of things, is unattainable? By no means. There is nothing dreary about Housman. If Christianity gives hope, strength and promise, paganism gives its own brand of fortitude and consolation. Profoundly melancholy as it often is, it never droops; it is sad and ironic, but never cynical—at least, about humanity. Man in his poems is fighting a rearguard action for a lost cause. He must be armoured against fate. All his beauty and bravery will not save him, but it is good to have these things.

If there is much pessimism and melancholy in him there is much fortitude and courage:

> If here to-day the cloud of thunder lours
>   To-morrow it will hie on far behests;
> The flesh will grieve on other bones than ours
>   Soon, and the soul will mourn in other breasts.
>
> The troubles of our proud and angry dust
>   Are from eternity, and shall not fail.
> Bear them we can, and if we can we must.
>   Shoulder the sky, my lad, and drink your ale.
>
> (No. 50)

In his Preface to the first volume of Manilius in 1903 Housman wrote: 'How the world is managed, and why it was created, I cannot tell; but it is no feather-bed for the repose of sluggards.'

If atheism takes away immortal hope, it gives other things: the eye looks with a keener glance at transitory beauty: it sees more sharply the splendour as well as the pathos of human effort; it loves things more because they die.

It is because of this feeling that Housman's craving for friendship is so strong, his poems on friendship so many. His most unusual poem, the long four-beat *Hell Gate* (**LP XXXI*), is nothing but an allegory of friendship which can cheat Hell itself. The sentry at the gate of Hell, 'in his finery of fire', is none other than our old friend Ned from Shropshire. In Marlowe's *Faustus* Mephistopheles said to Faust:

> *Solamen miseris socios habuisse doloris*

—'it is a consolation to the wretched to have had companions in pain'.

Mephistopheles was talking about society in Hell; but *mutatis mutandis*, this will do for Housman's 'too-much loved earth'.

In sending a poem (*Illic Jacet*) to his sister on the death of her son at Loos in 1915, Housman wrote that it is the 'business of poetry to harmonise the sadness of the universe'. This, in the end, is the secret of Housman's appeal: whether we say that he has given beauty to sadness or sadness to beauty (and he has done both), the formal perfection of his statement of a view of life implies a control over the raw stuff which surrounds us. He speaks both to the mind and heart. It is not necessary to believe in the philosophy his poems embody to be deeply moved by them, any more than it is necessary to be a Christian to enjoy *Paradise Lost* or a pagan to enjoy Lucretius. (Housman himself thought that Christian poetry could best be enjoyed by an unbeliever.) In *The Name and Nature of Poetry* he speaks of the appeal of poetry to 'something in man which is obscure and latent, something older than the present organisation of his nature'. He is able to make this appeal himself, in music and meaning: in meaning, because he deals with the fundamentals of the human lot, in music in a way that may not be analysable, but which is experienced. He passes his own test: we recognise his as poetry by the excited symptoms it provokes in us.

A Biographical Outline

(Passages in inverted commas, unless otherwise ascribed, are from Housman's letter of 1933 in reply to a questionnaire from M. Maurice Pollet.)

1859   Alfred Edward Housman born, the son of a solicitor, at Fockbury, Worcestershire. Followed within the next nine years by four brothers and two sisters, a family of which he was the leading spirit in play, and, to a certain extent, instruction.

1860   The family removed to Perry Hall, Bromsgrove, in Worcestershire.

        'I was brought up in the Church of England and in the High Church party.'

1870   (September) Became a Foundation Scholar at Bromsgrove School.

        'I had a sentimental feeling for Shropshire because its hills were our western horizon.'

        'I did not know the country well, except in parts, and some of my topographical details are wrong and imaginary' (letter of 14 April 1934 to Houston Martin, a young graduate of Yale).

1870   Death of his mother on his twelfth birthday.

1872   'I became a Deist.'

1877 Entered St John's College, Oxford, on an open scholarship of £100 a year, to read Greats.

1879 Took a First in Honour Moderations.

1880 ['I became] an atheist.'

1880–1 Shared rooms with two contemporaries, A. W. Pollard, who took a First in History in 1881, and Moses Jackson, a scientist, who took a First, both scholars of St John's.

'Oxford had not much effect on me, except that I there met my greatest friend.'

1881 Failed his final examination, and left Oxford without a degree.

Various reasons have been assigned for this preposterous result—that he was not interested in the ancient history and philosophical part of his course, that he thought he could get by on his knowledge of literature, that the teaching at St John's was poor. The simplest explanation is his own to his friend, A. S. F. Gow, long later, that his examiners had no option but to plough him; he had shown up no answers to many of the questions set. This is a failure apt to be fatal to examinees. However, this only puts the puzzle further back: why these blanks? Many critics have seen the explanation in unhappiness engendered by a hopeless affection for Moses Jackson.

Many years later he told his brother Laurence that Jackson 'was the man who had more influence on my life than anybody else'. In going through his brother's correspondence after his death, Laurence found an envelope endorsed 'Mo's last letter'. 'The letter had been written faintly, in the hospital where Jackson died soon after; and above the faint writing the better to preserve it (keeping the form of each letter carefully), Alfred had himself gone over the whole in ink.' (Related in *A.E.H.*). Housman himself told Jackson that he thought more of him than anything in the world, and said: 'You are largely responsible for my writing poetry and you ought to take the consequences'.[1] The first volume of *Manilius* (1903) was dedicated to Jackson in noble elegiacs.

This devotion to Jackson—

> This long and sure-set liking,
> This boundless will to please—

seems to have been the greatest emotional experience of Housman's life, and it seems likely that it found some reflection in his poetry and perhaps coloured his view of life. There is nothing overtly personal in the poems published in his lifetime; but two in *More Poems*, Nos. *XXXI* and No. 93, seem to speak more painfully of personal emotional disaster than any others he wrote. Rough drafts of No. *XXXI*—

> Because I liked you better
> Than suits a man to say,
> It irked you, and I promised
> To throw the thought away—

[1] Quoted by George L. Watson, *A. E. Housman: A Divided Life* (Hart-Davis).

39

occur in Housman's earliest notebook (A), which contains one poem as early as 1890, though we do not know the precise date of No. *XXXI—the poem in question.

1881 (May) to 1882 (December) teaching at Bromsgrove School, and preparing for Civil Service examinations. 'He came back from Oxford a changed character' (Laurence, in *A.E.H.*); and his sister Mrs Symons describes him as 'a stricken and petrified brother, who, from that time, was withdrawn from all of us behind an impenetrable barrier of reserve'.

1882 Clerk in the Patent Office, where Jackson was already a clerk, at a salary of £100 a year. Spent the evenings reading Greek and Latin literature in the British Museum.

1882–6 Shared lodgings in the Bayswater Road with Jackson and his younger brother Adalbert.

1882 His first published paper (on Horace) in the *Journal of Philology*.

1886 Removed to Byron Cottage, Hampstead, where he lived on his own for 19 years.

1887 Jackson went to Karachi, India, as Principal of a Training College. The two kept up a correspondence, and saw each other on Jackson's leaves; later on, Housman became godfather to one of Jackson's four sons.

1889 Jackson returned to London to marry. (Six years later, Housman started an *Epithalamium*, but it was 27 years before he finished it and published it as *LP *XXIV*.)

1889 Death of Adalbert (see *MP *XLII*).

1892   Became Professor of Latin at University College, London—'rescued from the gutter', as he put it. His application for the post was supported by 17 scholars in Europe and America.

1896   (late February or early March) *A Shropshire Lad* published (500 copies).

1898   (14 September) Second edition of *A Shropshire Lad* (500 copies).

1901   (30 October) Death of youngest brother, George Herbert, in the Boer War (see No. 58 and *MP *XL*).

1903   Edition of the *Astronomica* of Manilius, Book I. Housman did not conceal his low opinion of the poet whom he spent many years of his life editing. He called him 'a facile and frivolous poet, the brightest facet of whose genius was an eminent aptitude for doing sums in verse' (quoted from Gow), and said that 'when he came to write his fifth book, [he] no longer possessed even so much astronomy as had sufficed him for writing his first'. The last of the five volumes came out in 1930. All were published at Housman's own expense and sold well below cost price. 'But this unscrupulous artifice', he wrote in the Preface to Volume V, 'did not overcome the natural disrelish of mankind for the combination of a tedious author with an odious editor.' One is tempted to call this boring chore an instance of Housman's masochism, but in reality it was a choice of work in which he thought he could excel (see Appendix II, 2(b).) 'A textual critic, engaged upon his business,' he wrote, 'is not at all like Newton investigating the motions of the planets: he is much more like a dog hunting for fleas. If a dog hunted for fleas on mathematical principles, he would never catch a flea, except by accident.' . . . To be a good textual critic 'one thing beyond all others is necessary; and that is, to have a head, not a pump-kin, on your shoulders, and brains, not pudding, in your head'.

(The dedication in Latin elegiacs to Moses Jackson, for whom he had a morocco-bound, gilt-edged copy made, was enthusiastically re-viewed by H. E. Butler as 'a unique combination—a very perfect poet and the greatest Latin scholar of modern times'.)[1]

1905   Edition of Juvenal.

1911–36   Made Professor of Latin at Cambridge, with a fellowship at Trinity College. The electors to the Chair did not ask for testimonials; and, as Gow drily remarks, since 'Housman by this time had applied his lash to most of the eminent living Latinists, it is perhaps as well' that they did not.

1911   Accepted an offer of an Honorary Fellowship at his old college, St John's, Oxford.

1921   (4 August) Lecture to the Classical Association: *The Application of Thought to Textual Criticism* (quota-tions from this are made under the entry for 1903 above).

1922   (19 October) Publication of *Last Poems* (4,000 copies).

1923   (14 January) Death of Moses Jackson in Vancouver.

1926   Edition of Lucan.

[1] Review of *Poems in Latin*, compiled by John Sparrow, 1941 (R.E.S.), Vol. 19, 1943.

1929   Refused the offer of the O.M.
1933   (9 May) Leslie Stephen lecture: *The Name and Nature of Poetry* (see Appendix II, 3).
1935   In a Cambridge nursing home, for a few weeks.
1936   (18 March) Gave his last lecture. Refused the office of Poet Laureate.
1936   (26 October) Died.

His ashes were buried outside the north wall of Ludlow Parish Church, with a tablet above the grave, with, among other details, three lines from the poem (No. 99) he had written long ago in 1881, when he was an undergraduate:

> Good-night; ensured release,
> Imperishable peace,
> Have these for yours.

1936   *More Poems* published (8,586 copies). Second impression of *More Poems* (5,081 copies). Third impression (7,500 copies).
1939   *The Collected Poems* (Jonathan Cape).

There is a passage of introspective analysis in the book of another unusual man, T. E. Lawrence: against this passage quoted in a series of *Seven Pillars of Wisdom*, Housman wrote: 'This is me'. Here is the passage:

'There was a craving to be liked—so strong and nervous that never could I open myself friendly to another. The terror of failure in an effort so important made me shrink from trying; besides, there was the standard; for intimacy seemed shameful, unless the other could make the perfect reply in the same language, after the same method, for the same reasons.

'There was a craving to be famous; and a horror of being known to like being known. Contempt for my passion for distinction made me refuse every offered honour.'

Poems

1

Loveliest of trees, the cherry now
Is hung with bloom along the bough,
And stands about the woodland ride
Wearing white for Eastertide.

Now, of my threescore years and ten,
Twenty will not come again,
And take from seventy springs a score,
It only leaves me fifty more.

And since to look at things in bloom
Fifty springs are little room,
About the woodlands I will go
To see the cherry hung with snow.

2

THE RECRUIT

Leave your home behind, lad,
  And reach your friends your hand,
And go, and luck go with you
  While Ludlow tower shall stand.

Oh, come you home of Sunday
  When Ludlow streets are still
And Ludlow bells are calling
  To farm and lane and mill,

Or come you home of Monday
  When Ludlow market hums
And Ludlow chimes are playing
  'The conquering hero comes',

Come you home a hero,
  Or come not home at all,
The lads you leave will mind you
  Till Ludlow tower shall fall.

And you will list the bugle
  That blows in lands of morn,
And make the foes of England
  Be sorry you were born.

And you till trump of doomsday
  On lands of morn may lie,
And make the hearts of comrades
  Be heavy where you die.

Leave your home behind you,
  Your friends by field and town:
Oh, town and field will mind you
  Till Ludlow tower is down.

3

REVEILLE

Wake: the silver dusk returning
  Up the beach of darkness brims,
And the ship of sunrise burning
  Strands upon the eastern rims.

Wake: the vaulted shadow shatters,
  Trampled to the floor it spanned,
And the tent of night in tatters
  Straws the sky-pavilioned land.

Up, lad, up, 'tis late for lying:
  Hear the drums of morning play;
Hark, the empty highways crying
  'Who'll beyond the hills away?'

Towns and countries woo together,
  Forelands beacon, belfries call;
Never lad that trod on leather
  Lived to feast his heart with all.

Up, lad: thews that lie and cumber
  Sunlit pallets never thrive;
Morns abed and daylight slumber
  Were not meant for man alive.

Clay lies still, but blood's a rover;
    Breath's a ware that will not keep.
Up, lad: when the journey's over
    There'll be time enough to sleep.

4

Oh see how thick the goldcup flowers
  Are lying in field and lane,
With dandelions to tell the hours
  That never are told again.
Oh may I squire you round the meads
  And pick you posies gay?
—'Twill do no harm to take my arm.
  'You may, young man, you may.'

Ah, spring was sent for lass and lad,
  'Tis now the blood runs gold,
And man and maid had best be glad
  Before the world is old.
What flowers to-day may flower to-morrow,
  But never as good as new.
—Suppose I wound my arm right round—
  ' 'Tis true, young man, 'tis true.'

Some lads there are, 'tis shame to say,
  That only court to thieve,
And once they bear the bloom away
  'Tis little enough they leave.
Then keep your heart for men like me
  And safe from trustless chaps.
My love is true and all for you.
  'Perhaps, young man, perhaps.'

Oh, look in my eyes then, can you doubt?
　　—Why, 'tis a mile from town.
How green the grass is all about!
　　We might as well sit down.
—Ah, life, what is it but a flower?
　　Why must true lovers sigh?
Be kind, have pity, my own, my pretty,—
　　'Good-bye, young man, good-bye.'

5

When smoke stood up from Ludlow,
  And mist blew off from Teme,
And blithe afield to ploughing
  Against the morning beam
  I strode beside my team,

The blackbird in the coppice
  Looked out to see me stride,
And hearkened as I whistled
  The trampling team beside,
  And fluted and replied:

'Lie down, lie down, young yeoman;
  What use to rise and rise?
Rise man a thousand mornings
  Yet down at last he lies,
  And then the man is wise.'

I heard the tune he sang me,
  And spied his yellow bill;
I picked a stone and aimed it
  And threw it with a will:
  Then the bird was still.

Then my soul within me
  Took up the blackbird's strain,
And still beside the horses
  Along the dewy lane
  It sang the song again:

'Lie down, lie down, young yeoman;
  The sun moves always west;
The road one treads to labour
  Will lead one home to rest,
  And that will be the best.'

'Farewell to barn and stack and tree,
  Farewell to Severn shore.
Terence, look your last at me,
  For I come home no more.

'The sun burns on the half-mown hill,
  By now the blood is dried;
And Maurice amongst the hay lies still
  And my knife is in his side.

'My mother thinks us long away;
  'Tis time the field were mown.
She had two sons at rising day,
  To-night she'll be alone.

'And here's a bloody hand to shake,
  And oh, man, here's good-bye;
We'll sweat no more on scythe and rake,
  My bloody hands and I.

'I wish you strength to bring you pride,
  And a love to keep you clean,
And I wish you luck, come Lammastide,
  At racing on the green.

'Long for me the rick will wait,
  And long will wait the fold,
And long will stand the empty plate,
  And dinner will be cold.'

On moonlit heath and lonesome bank
  The sheep beside me graze;
And yon the gallows used to clank
  Fast by the four cross ways.

A careless shepherd once would keep
  The flocks by moonlight there,[1]
And high amongst the glimmering sheep
  The dead man stood on air.

They hang us now in Shrewsbury jail:
  The whistles blow forlorn,
And trains all night groan on the rail
  To men that die at morn.

There sleeps in Shrewsbury jail to-night,
  Or wakes, as may betide,
A better lad, if things went right,
  Than most that sleep outside.

And naked to the hangman's noose
  The morning clocks will ring
A neck God made for other use
  Than strangling in a string.

[1] Hanging in chains was called keeping sheep by moonlight.

And sharp the link of life will snap,
    And dead on air will stand
Heels that held up as straight a chap
    As treads upon the land.

So here I'll watch the night and wait
    To see the morning shine,
When he will hear the stroke of eight
    And not the stroke of nine;

And wish my friend as sound a sleep
    As lads' I did not know,
That shepherded the moonlit sheep
    A hundred years ago.

MARCH

The Sun at noon to higher air,
Unharnessing the silver Pair
That late before his chariot swam,
Rides on the gold wool of the Ram.

So braver notes the storm-cock sings
To start the rusted wheel of things,
And brutes in field and brutes in pen
Leap that the world goes round again.

The boys are up the woods with day
To fetch the daffodils away,
And home at noonday from the hills
They bring no dearth of daffodils.

Afield for palms the girls repair,
And sure enough the palms are there,
And each will find by hedge or pond
Her waving silver-tufted wand.

In farm and field through all the shire
The eye beholds the heart's desire;
Ah, let not only mine be vain,
For lovers should be loved again.

9

When I watch the living meet,
  And the moving pageant file
Warm and breathing through the street
  Where I lodge a little while,

If the heats of hate and lust
  In the house of flesh are strong,
Let me mind the house of dust
  Where my sojourn shall be long.

In the nation that is not
  Nothing stands that stood before;
There revenges are forgot,
  And the hater hates no more;

Lovers lying two and two
  Ask not whom they sleep beside,
And the bridegroom all night through
  Never turns him to the bride.

10

When I was one-and-twenty
  I heard a wise man say,
'Give crowns and pounds and guineas,
  But not your heart away;
Give pearls away and rubies
  But keep your fancy free.'
But I was one-and-twenty,
  No use to talk to me.

When I was one-and-twenty
  I heard him say again,
'The heart out of the bosom
  Was never given in vain;
'Tis paid with sighs a plenty
  And sold for endless rue.'
And I am two-and-twenty,
  And oh, 'tis true, 'tis true.

There pass the careless people
   That call their souls their own:
Here by the road I loiter,
   How idle and alone.

Ah, past the plunge of plummet,
   In seas I cannot sound,
My heart and soul and senses,
   World without end, are drowned.

His folly has not fellow
   Beneath the blue of day
That gives to man or woman
   His heart and soul away.

There flowers no balm to sain him
   From east of earth to west
That's lost for everlasting
   The heart out of his breast.

Here by the labouring highway
   With empty hands I stroll:
Sea-deep, till doomsday morning,
   Lie lost my heart and soul.

12

It nods and curtseys and recovers
    When the wind blows above,
The nettle on the graves of lovers
    That hanged themselves for love.

The nettle nods, the wind blows over,
    The man, he does not move,
The lover of the grave, the lover
    That hanged himself for love.

TO AN ATHLETE DYING YOUNG

The time you won your town the race
We chaired you through the market-place;
Man and boy stood cheering by,
And home we brought you shoulder-high.

To-day, the road all runners come,
Shoulder-high we bring you home,
And set you at your threshold down,
Townsman of a stiller town.

Smart lad, to slip betimes away
From fields where glory does not stay
And early though the laurel grows
It withers quicker than the rose.

Eyes the shady night has shut
Cannot see the record cut,
And silence sounds no worse than cheers
After earth has stopped the ears:

Now you will not swell the rout
Of lads that wore their honours out.
Runners whom renown outran
And the name died before the man.

So set, before its echoes fade,
The fleet foot on the sill of shade,
And hold to the low lintel up
The still-defended challenge-cup.

And round that early-laurelled head
Will flock to gaze the strengthless dead,
And find unwithered on its curls
The garland briefer than a girl's.

14

Oh fair enough are sky and plain,
  But I know fairer far:
Those are as beautiful again
  That in the water are;

The pools and rivers wash so clean
  The trees and clouds and air,
The like on earth was never seen,
  And oh that I were there.

These are the thoughts I often think
  As I stand gazing down
In act upon the cressy brink
  To strip and dive and drown;

But in the golden-sanded brooks
  And azure meres I spy
A silly lad that longs and looks
  And wishes he were I.

BREDON[1] HILL

In summertime on Bredon
  The bells they sound so clear;
Round both the shires they ring them
  In steeples far and near,
  A happy noise to hear.

Here of a Sunday morning
  My love and I would lie,
And see the coloured counties,
  And hear the larks so high
  About us in the sky.

The bells would ring to call her
  In valleys miles away:
'Come all to church, good people;
  Good people, come and pray.'
  But here my love would stay.

And I would turn and answer
  Among the springing thyme,
'Oh, peal upon our wedding,
  And we will hear the chime,
  And come to church in time.'

[1] Pronounced Breedon.

But when the snows at Christmas
    On Bredon top were strown,
My love rose up so early
    And stole out unbeknown
    And went to church alone.

They tolled the one bell only,
    Groom there was none to see,
The mourners followed after,
    And so to church went she,
    And would not wait for me.

The bells they sound on Bredon,
    And still the steeples hum.
'Come all to church, good people,'—
    Oh, noisy bells, be dumb;
    I hear you, I will come.

The lads in their hundreds to Ludlow come in for the fair,
   There's men from the barn and the forge and the mill
     and the fold,
The lads for the girls and the lads for the liquor are there,
   And there with the rest are the lads that will never be
     old.

There's chaps from the town and the field and the till and
     the cart,
   And many to count are the stalwart, and many the
     brave,
And many the handsome of face and the handsome of
     heart,
   And few that will carry their looks or their truth to the
     grave.

I wish one could know them, I wish there were tokens to
     tell
   The fortunate fellows that now you can never discern;
And then one could talk with them friendly and wish
     them farewell
   And watch them depart on the way that they will not
     return.

But now you may stare as you like and there's nothing to
     scan;
   And brushing your elbow unguessed-at and not to be
     told
They carry back bright to the coiner the mintage of man,
   The lads that will die in their glory and never be old.

Along the field as we came by
A year ago, my love and I,
The aspen over stile and stone
Was talking to itself alone.
'Oh who are these that kiss and pass?
A country lover and his lass;
Two lovers looking to be wed;
And time shall put them both to bed,
But she shall lie with earth above,
And he beside another love.'

And sure enough beneath the tree
There walks another love with me,
And overhead the aspen heaves
Its rainy-sounding silver leaves;
And I spell nothing in their stir,
But now perhaps they speak to her,
And plain for her to understand
They talk about a time at hand
When I shall sleep with clover clad,
And she beside another lad.

'Is my team ploughing,
    That I was used to drive
And hear the harness jingle
    When I was man alive?'

Ay, the horses trample,
    The harness jingles now;
No change though you lie under
    The land you used to plough.

'Is football playing
    Along the river shore,
With lads to chase the leather,
    Now I stand up no more?'

Ay, the ball is flying,
    The lads play heart and soul;
The goal stands up, the keeper
    Stands up to keep the goal.

'Is my girl happy,
    That I thought hard to leave,
And has she tired of weeping
    As she lies down at eve?'

Ay, she lies down lightly,
    She lies not down to weep:
Your girl is well contented.
    Be still, my lad, and sleep.

'Is my friend hearty,
   Now I am thin and pine,
And has he found to sleep in
   A better bed than mine?'

Yes, lad, I lie easy,
   I lie as lads would choose;
I cheer a dead man's sweetheart,
   Never ask me whose.

THE WELSH MARCHES

High the vanes of Shrewsbury gleam
Islanded in Severn stream;
The bridges from the steepled crest
Cross the water east and west.

The flag of morn in conqueror's state
Enters at the English gate:
The vanquished eve, as night prevails,
Bleeds upon the road to Wales.

Ages since the vanquished bled
Round my mother's marriage-bed;
There the ravens feasted far
About the open house of war:

When Severn down to Buildwas ran
Coloured with the death of man,
Couched upon her brother's grave
The Saxon got me on the slave.

The sound of fight is silent long
That began the ancient wrong;
Long the voice of tears is still
That wept of old the endless ill.

In my heart it has not died,
The war that sleeps on Severn side;
They cease not fighting, east and west,
On the marches of my breast.

Here the truceless armies yet
Trample, rolled in blood and sweat;
They kill and kill and never die;
And I think that each is I.

None will part us, none undo
The knot that makes one flesh of two,
Sick with hatred, sick with pain,
Strangling—When shall we be slain?

When shall I be dead and rid
Of the wrong my father did?
How long, how long, till spade and hearse
Put to sleep my mother's curse?

THE LENT LILY

'Tis spring; come out to ramble
　The hilly brakes around,
For under thorn and bramble
　About the hollow ground
　The primroses are found.

And there's the windflower chilly
　With all the winds at play,
And there's the Lenten lily
　That has not long to stay
　And dies on Easter day.

And since till girls go maying
　You find the primrose still,
And find the windflower playing
　With every wind at will,
　But not the daffodil,

Bring baskets now, and sally
　Upon the spring's array,
And bear from hill and valley
　The daffodil away
　That dies on Easter day.

21

Others, I am not the first,
Have willed more mischief than they durst:
If in the breathless night I too
Shiver now, 'tis nothing new.

More than I, if truth were told,
Have stood and sweated hot and cold,
And through their reins in ice and fire
Fear contended with desire.

Agued once like me were they,
But I like them shall win my way
Lastly to the bed of mould
Where there's neither heat nor cold.

But from my grave across my brow
Plays no wind of healing now,
And fire and ice within me fight
Beneath the suffocating night.

On Wenlock Edge the wood's in trouble;
　His forest fleece the Wrekin heaves;
The gale, it plies the saplings double,
　And thick on Severn snow the leaves.

'Twould blow like this through holt and hanger
　When Uricon the city stood:
'Tis the old wind in the old anger,
　But then it threshed another wood.

Then, 'twas before my time, the Roman
　At yonder heaving hill would stare:
The blood that warms an English yeoman,
　The thoughts that hurt him, they were there.

There, like the wind through woods in riot,
　Through him the gale of life blew high;
The tree of man was never quiet:
　Then 'twas the Roman, now 'tis I.

The gale, it plies the saplings double,
　It blows so hard, 'twill soon be gone:
To-day the Roman and his trouble
　Are ashes under Uricon.

From far, from eve and morning
  And yon twelve-winded sky,
The stuff of life to knit me
  Blew hither: here am I.

Now—for a breath I tarry
  Nor yet disperse apart—
Take my hand quick and tell me,
  What have you in your heart.

Speak now, and I will answer;
  How shall I help you, say;
Ere to the wind's twelve quarters
  I take my endless way.

If truth in hearts that perish
   Could move the powers on high,
I think the love I bear you
   Should make you not to die.

Sure, sure, if stedfast meaning,
   If single thought could save,
The world might end to-morrow,
   You should not see the grave.

This long and sure-set liking,
   This boundless will to please,
—Oh, you should live for ever
   If there were help in these.

But now, since all is idle,
   To this lost heart be kind,
Ere to a town you journey
   Where friends are ill to find.

On the idle hill of summer,
  Sleepy with the flow of streams,
Far I hear the steady drummer
  Drumming like a noise in dreams.

Far and near and low and louder
  On the roads of earth go by,
Dear to friends and food for powder,
  Soldiers marching, all to die.

East and west on fields forgotten
  Bleach the bones of comrades slain,
Lovely lads and dead and rotten;
  None that go return again.

Far the calling bugles hollo,
  High the screaming fife replies,
Gay the files of scarlet follow:
  Woman bore me, I will rise.

26

White in the moon the long road lies,
  The moon stands blank above;
White in the moon the long road lies
  That leads me from my love.

Still hangs the hedge without a gust,
  Still, still the shadows stay:
My feet upon the moonlit dust
  Pursue the ceaseless way.

The world is round, so travellers tell,
  And straight though reach the track,
Trudge on, trudge on, 'twill all be well,
  The way will guide one back.

But ere the circle homeward hies
  Far, far must it remove:
White in the moon the long road lies
  That leads me from my love.

As through the wild green hills of Wyre
The train ran, changing sky and shire,
And far behind, a fading crest,
Low in the forsaken west
Sank the high-reared head of Clee,
My hand lay empty on my knee.
Aching on my knee it lay:
That morning half a shire away
So many an honest fellow's fist
Had well-nigh wrung it from the wrist.
Hand, said I, since now we part
From fields and men we know by heart,
For strangers' faces, strangers' lands,—
Hand, you have held true fellows' hands.
Be clean then; rot before you do
A thing they'd not believe of you.
You and I must keep from shame
In London streets the Shropshire name;
On banks of Thames they must not say
Severn breeds worse men than they;
And friends abroad must bear in mind
Friends at home they leave behind.
Oh, I shall be stiff and cold
When I forget you, hearts of gold;
The land where I shall mind you not
Is the land where all's forgot.
And if my foot returns no more
To Teme nor Corve nor Severn shore,

Luck, my lads, be with you still
By falling stream and standing hill,
By chiming tower and whispering tree,
Men that made a man of me.
About your work in town and farm
Still you'll keep my head from harm,
Still you'll help me, hands that gave
A grasp to friend me to the grave.

The winds out of the west land blow,
  My friends have breathed them there;
Warm with the blood of lads I know
  Comes east the sighing air.

It fanned their temples, filled their lungs,
  Scattered their forelocks free;
My friends made words of it with tongues
  That talk no more to me.

Their voices, dying as they fly,
  Loose on the wind are sown;
The names of men blow soundless by,
  My fellows' and my own.

Oh lads, at home I heard you plain,
  But here your speech is still,
And down the sighing wind in vain
  You hollo from the hill.

The wind and I, we both were there,
  But neither long abode;
Now through the friendless world we fare
  And sigh upon the road.

29

'Tis time, I think, by Wenlock town
   The golden broom should blow;
The hawthorn sprinkled up and down
   Should charge the land with snow.

Spring will not wait the loiterer's time
   Who keeps so long away;
So others wear the broom and climb
   The hedgerows heaped with may.

Oh tarnish late on Wenlock Edge,
   Gold that I never see;
Lie long, high snowdrifts in the hedge
   That will not shower on me.

30

Into my heart an air that kills
    From yon far country blows:
What are those blue remembered hills,
    What spires, what farms are those?

That is the land of lost content,
    I see it shining plain,
The happy highways where I went
    And cannot come again.

In my own shire, if I was sad,
Homely comforters I had:
The earth, because my heart was sore,
Sorrowed for the son she bore;
And standing hills, long to remain,
Shared their short-lived comrade's pain.
And bound for the same bourn as I,
On every road I wandered by,
Trod beside me, close and dear,
The beautiful and death-struck year:
Whether in the woodland brown
I heard the beechnut rustle down,
And saw the purple crocus pale
Flower about the autumn dale;
Or littering far the fields of May
Lady-smocks a-bleaching lay,
And like a skylit water stood
The bluebells in the azured wood.

Yonder, lightening other loads,
The seasons range the country roads,
But here in London streets I ken
No such helpmates, only men;
And these are not in plight to bear,
If they would, another's care.
They have enough as 'tis: I see
In many an eye that measures me

The mortal sickness of a mind
Too unhappy to be kind.
Undone with misery, all they can
Is to hate their fellow man;
And till they drop they needs must still
Look at you and wish you ill.

32

THE MERRY GUIDE

Once in the wind of morning
  I ranged the thymy wold;
The world-wide air was azure
  And all the brooks ran gold.

There through the dews beside me
  Behold a youth that trod,
With feathered cap on forehead,
  And poised a golden rod.

With mien to match the morning
  And gay delightful guise
And friendly brows and laughter
  He looked me in the eyes.

Oh whence, I asked, and whither?
  He smiled and would not say,
And looked at me and beckoned
  And laughed and led the way.

And with kind looks and laughter
  And nought to say beside
We two went on together,
  I and my happy guide.

Across the glittering pastures
　　And empty upland still
And solitude of shepherds
　　High in the folded hill,

By hanging woods and hamlets
　　That gaze through orchards down
On many a windmill turning
　　And far-discovered town,

With gay regards of promise
　　And sure unslackened stride
And smiles and nothing spoken
　　Led on my merry guide.

By blowing realms of woodland
　　With sunstruck vanes afield
And cloud-led shadows sailing
　　About the windy weald,

By valley-guarded granges
　　And silver waters wide,
Content at heart I followed
　　With my delightful guide.

And like the cloudy shadows
　　Across the country blown
We two fare on for ever,
　　But not we two alone.

With the great gale we journey
   That breathes from gardens thinned,
Borne in the drift of blossoms
   Whose petals throng the wind;

Buoyed on the heaven-heard whisper
   Of dancing leaflets whirled
From all the woods that autumn
   Bereaves in all the world.

And midst the fluttering legion
   Of all that ever died
I follow, and before us
   Goes the delightful guide,

With lips that brim with laughter
   But never once respond,
And feet that fly on feathers,
   And serpent-circled wand.

THE IMMORTAL PART

When I meet the morning beam
Or lay me down at night to dream,
I hear my bones within me say,
'Another night, another day.

'When shall this slough of sense be cast,
This dust of thoughts be laid at last,
The man of flesh and soul be slain
And the man of bone remain?

'This tongue that talks, these lungs that shout,
These thews that hustle us about,
This brain that fills the skull with schemes,
And its humming hive of dreams,—

'These to-day are proud in power
And lord it in their little hour:
The immortal bones obey control
Of dying flesh and dying soul.

''Tis long till eve and morn are gone:
Slow the endless night comes on,
And late to fulness grows the birth
That shall last as long as earth.

'Wanderers eastward, wanderers west,
Know you why you cannot rest?
'Tis that every mother's son
Travails with a skeleton.

'Lie down in the bed of dust;
Bear the fruit that bear you must;
Bring the eternal seed to light,
And morn is all the same as night.

'Rest you so from trouble sore,
Fear the heat o' the sun no more,
Nor the snowing winter wild,
Now you labour not with child.

'Empty vessel, garment cast,
We that wore you long shall last.
—Another night, another day.'
So my bones within me say.

Therefore they shall do my will
To-day while I am master still,
And flesh and soul, now both are strong,
Shall hale the sullen slaves along,

Before this fire of sense decay,
This smoke of thought blow clean away,
And leave with ancient night alone
The stedfast and enduring bone.

THE CARPENTER'S SON

'Here the hangman stops his cart:
Now the best of friends must part.
Fare you well, for ill fare I:
Live, lads, and I will die.

'Oh, at home had I but stayed
'Prenticed to my father's trade,
Had I stuck to plane and adze,
I had not been lost, my lads.

'Then I might have built perhaps
Gallows-trees for other chaps,
Never dangled on my own,
Had I but left ill alone.

'Now, you see, they hang me high,
And the people passing by
Stop to shake their fists and curse;
So 'tis come from ill to worse.

'Here hang I, and right and left
Two poor fellows hang for theft:
All the same's the luck we prove,
Though the midmost hangs for love.

'Comrades all, that stand and gaze,
Walk henceforth in other ways;
See my neck and save your own:
Comrades all, leave ill alone.

'Make some day a decent end,
Shrewder fellows than your friend.
Fare you well, for ill fare I:
Live, lads, and I will die.'

Be still, my soul, be still; the arms you bear are brittle,
  Earth and high heaven are fixt of old and founded
    strong.
'Think rather,—call to thought, if now you grieve a little,
  The days when we had rest, O soul, for they were long.

Men loved unkindness then, but lightless in the quarry
  I slept and saw not; tears fell down, I did not mourn;
Sweat ran and blood sprang out and I was never sorry:
  Then it was well with me, in days ere I was born.

Now, and I muse for why and never find the reason,
  I pace the earth, and drink the air, and feel the sun.
Be still, be still, my soul; it is but for a season:
  Let us endure an hour and see injustice done.

Ay, look: high heaven and earth ail from the prime foun-
  dation;
  All thoughts to rive the heart are here, and all are vain:
Horror and scorn and hate and fear and indignation—
  Oh why did I awake? when shall I sleep again?

> *Clunton and Clunbury,*
> *Clungunford and Clun,*
> *Are the quietest places*
> *Under the sun.*

In valleys of springs of rivers,
    By Ony and Teme and Clun,
The country for easy livers,
    The quietest under the sun,

We still had sorrows to lighten,
    One could not be always glad,
And lads knew trouble at Knighton
    When I was a Knighton lad.

By bridges that Thames runs under
    In London, the town built ill,
'Tis sure small matter for wonder
    If sorrow is with one still.

And if as a lad grows older
    The troubles he bears are more,
He carries his griefs on a shoulder
    That handselled them long before.

Where shall one halt to deliver
    This luggage I'd lief set down?
Not Thames, not Teme is the river,
    Nor London nor Knighton the town:

'Tis a long way further than Knighton,
  A quieter place than Clun,
Where doomsday may thunder and lighten
  And little 'twill matter to one.

Far in a western brookland
  That bred me long ago
The poplars stand and tremble
  By pools I used to know.

There, in the windless night-time,
  The wanderer, marvelling why,
Halts on the bridge to hearken
  How soft the poplars sigh.

He hears: no more remembered
  In fields where I was known,
Here I lie down in London
  And turn to rest alone.

There, by the starlit fences,
  The wanderer halts and hears
My soul that lingers sighing
  About the glimmering weirs.

THE TRUE LOVER

The lad came to the door at night,
  When lovers crown their vows,
And whistled soft and out of sight
  In shadow of the boughs.

'I shall not vex you with my face
  Henceforth, my love, for aye;
So take me in your arms a space
  Before the east is grey.

'When I from hence away am past
  I shall not find a bride,
And you shall be the first and last
  I ever lay beside.'

She heard and went and knew not why;
  Her heart to his she laid;
Light was the air beneath the sky
  But dark under the shade.

'Oh do you breathe, lad, that your breast
  Seems not to rise and fall,
And here upon my bosom prest
  There beats no heart at all?'

'O loud, my girl, it once would knock,
  You should have felt it then;
But since for you I stopped the clock
  It never goes again.'

'Oh lad, what is it, lad, that drips
  Wet from your neck on mine?
What is it falling on my lips,
  My lad, that tastes of brine?'

'Oh like enough 'tis blood, my dear,
  For when the knife has slit
The throat across from ear to ear
  'Twill bleed because of it.'

Under the stars the air was light
  But dark below the boughs,
The still air of the speechless night,
  When lovers crown their vows.

With rue my heart is laden
  For golden friends I had,
For many a rose-lipt maiden
  And many a lightfoot lad.

By brooks too broad for leaping
  The lightfoot boys are laid;
The rose-lipt girls are sleeping
  In fields where roses fade.

Westward on the high-hilled plains
 Where for me the world began,
Still, I think, in newer veins
 Frets the changeless blood of man.

Now that other lads than I
 Strip to bathe on Severn shore,
They, no help, for all they try,
 Tread the mill I trod before.

There, when hueless is the west
 And the darkness hushes wide,
Where the lad lies down to rest
 Stands the troubled dream beside.

There, on thoughts that once were mine,
 Day looks down the eastern steep,
And the youth at morning shine
 Makes the vow he will not keep.

THE ISLE OF PORTLAND

The star-filled seas are smooth to-night
  From France to England strown;
Black towers above the Portland light
  The felon-quarried stone.

On yonder island, not to rise,
  Never to stir forth free,
Far from his folk a dead lad lies
  That once was friends with me.

Lie you easy, dream you light,
  And sleep you fast for aye;
And luckier may you find the night
  Than ever you found the day.

HUGHLEY STEEPLE

The vane on Hughley steeple
  Veers bright, a far-known sign,
And there lie Hughley people,
  And there lie friends of mine.
Tall in their midst the tower
  Divides the shade and sun,
And the clock strikes the hour
  And tells the time to none.

To south the headstones cluster,
  The sunny mounds lie thick;
The dead are more in muster
  At Hughley than the quick.
North, for a soon-told number,
  Chill graves the sexton delves,
And steeple-shadowed slumber
  The slayers of themselves.

To north, to south, lie parted,
  With Hughley tower above,
The kind, the single-hearted,
  The lads I used to love.
And, south or north, 'tis only
  A choice of friends one knows,
And I shall ne'er be lonely
  Asleep with these or those.

'Terence, this is stupid stuff:
You eat your victuals fast enough;
There can't be much amiss, 'tis clear,
To see the rate you drink your beer.
But oh, good Lord, the verse you make,
It gives a chap the belly-ache.
The cow, the old cow, she is dead;
It sleeps well, the horned head:
We poor lads, 'tis our turn now
To hear such tunes as killed the cow.
Pretty friendship 'tis to rhyme
Your friends to death before their time
Moping melancholy mad:
Come, pipe a tune to dance to, lad.'

Why, if 'tis dancing you would be,
There's brisker pipes than poetry.
Say, for what were hop-yards meant,
Or why was Burton built on Trent?
Oh many a peer of England brews
Livelier liquor than the Muse,
And malt does more than Milton can
To justify God's ways to man.
Ale, man, ale's the stuff to drink
For fellows whom it hurts to think:
Look into the pewter pot
To see the world as the world's not.
And faith, 'tis pleasant till 'tis past:
The mischief is that 'twill not last.

Oh I have been to Ludlow fair
And left my necktie God knows where,
And carried half-way home, or near,
Pints and quarts of Ludlow beer:
Then the world seemed none so bad,
And I myself a sterling lad;
And down in lovely muck I've lain,
Happy till I woke again.
Then I saw the morning sky:
Heigho, the tale was all a lie;
The world, it was the old world yet,
I was I, my things were wet,
And nothing now remained to do
But begin the game anew.

  Therefore, since the world has still
Much good, but much less good than ill,
And while the sun and moon endure
Luck's a chance, but trouble's sure,
I'd face it as a wise man would,
And train for ill and not for good.
'Tis true, the stuff I bring for sale
Is not so brisk a brew as ale:
Out of a stem that scored the hand
I wrung it in a weary land.
But take it: if the smack is sour,
The better for the embittered hour;
It should do good to heart and head
When your soul is in my soul's stead;
And I will friend you, if I may,
In the dark and cloudy day.

There was a king reigned in the East:
There, when kings will sit to feast,
They get their fill before they think
With poisoned meat and poisoned drink.
He gathered all that springs to birth
From the many-venomed earth;
First a little, thence to more,
He sampled all her killing store;
And easy, smiling, seasoned sound,
Sate the king when healths went round.
They put arsenic in his meat
And stared aghast to watch him eat;
They poured strychnine in his cup
And shook to see him drink it up:
They shook, they stared as white's their shirt:
Them it was their poison hurt.
—I tell the tale that I heard told.
Mithridates, he died old.

44

I hoed and trenched and weeded,
  And took the flowers to fair:
I brought them home unheeded;
  The hue was not the wear.

So up and down I sow them
  For lads like me to find,
When I shall lie below them,
  A dead man out of mind.

Some seed the birds devour,
  And some the season mars,
But here and there will flower
  The solitary stars,

And fields will yearly bear them
  As light-leaved spring comes on,
And luckless lads will wear them
  When I am dead and gone.

45

THE WEST

Beyond the moor and mountain crest
—Comrade, look not on the west—
The sun is down and drinks away
From air and land the lees of day.

The long cloud and the single pine
Sentinel the ending line,
And out beyond it, clear and wan,
Reach the gulfs of evening on.

The son of woman turns his brow
West from forty counties now,
And, as the edge of heaven he eyes,
Thinks eternal thoughts, and sighs.

Oh wide's the world, to rest or roam,
With change abroad and cheer at home,
Fights and furloughs, talk and tale,
Company and beef and ale.

But if I front the evening sky
Silent on the west look I,
And my comrade, stride for stride,
Paces silent at my side.

Comrade, look not on the west:
'Twill have the heart out of your breast;
'Twill take your thoughts and sink them far,
Leagues beyond the sunset bar.

Oh lad, I fear that yon's the sea
Where they fished for you and me,
And there, from whence we both were ta'en,
You and I shall drown again.

Send not on your soul before
To dive from that beguiling shore,
And let not yet the swimmer leave
His clothes upon the sands of eve.

Too fast to yonder strand forlorn
We journey, to the sunken bourn,
To flush the fading tinges eyed
By other lads at eventide.

Wide is the world, to rest or roam,
And early 'tis for turning home:
Plant your heel on earth and stand,
And let's forget our native land.

When you and I are spilt on air
Long we shall be strangers there;
Friends of flesh and bone are best:
Comrade, look not on the west.

46

As I gird on for fighting
　My sword upon my thigh,
I think on old ill fortunes
　Of better men than I.

Think I, the round world over,
　What golden lads are low
With hurts not mine to mourn for
　And shames I shall not know.

What evil luck soever
　For me remains in store,
'Tis sure much finer fellows
　Have fared much worse before.

So here are things to think on
　That ought to make me brave,
As I strap on for fighting
　My sword that will not save.

47

Her strong enchantments failing,
    Her towers of fear in wreck,
Her limbecks dried of poisons
    And the knife at her neck,

The Queen of air and darkness
    Begins to shrill and cry,
'O young man, O my slayer,
    To-morrow you shall die.'

O Queen of air and darkness,
    I think 'tis truth you say,
And I shall die to-morrow;
    But you will die to-day.

In valleys green and still
  Where lovers wander maying
They hear from over hill
  A music playing.

Behind the drum and fife,
  Past hawthornwood and hollow,
Through earth and out of life
  The soldiers follow.

The soldier's is the trade:
  In any wind or weather
He steals the heart of maid
  And man together.

The lover and his lass
  Beneath the hawthorn lying
Have heard the soldiers pass,
  And both are sighing.

And down the distance they
  With dying note and swelling
Walk the resounding way
  To the still dwelling.

Soldier from the wars returning,
  Spoiler of the taken town,
Here is ease that asks not earning;
  Turn you in and sit you down.

Peace is come and wars are over,
  Welcome you and welcome all,
While the charger crops the clover
  And his bridle hangs in stall.

Now no more of winters biting,
  Filth in trench from fall to spring,
Summers full of sweat and fighting
  For the Kesar or the King.

Rest you, charger, rust you, bridle;
  Kings and kesars, keep your pay;
Soldier, sit you down and idle
  At the inn of night for aye.

The chestnut casts his flambeaux, and the flowers
   Stream from the hawthorn on the wind away,
The doors clap to, the pane is blind with showers.
   Pass me the can, lad; there's an end of May.

There's one spoilt spring to scant our mortal lot,
One season ruined of our little store.
May will be fine next year as like as not:
   Oh ay, but then we shall be twenty-four.

We for a certainty are not the first
   Have sat in taverns while the tempest hurled
Their hopeful plans to emptiness, and cursed
   Whatever brute and blackguard made the world.

It is in truth iniquity on high
   To cheat our sentenced souls of aught they crave,
And mar the merriment as you and I
   Fare on our long fool's-errand to the grave.

Iniquity it is; but pass the can.
   My lad, no pair of kings our mothers bore;
Our only portion is the estate of man:
   We want the moon, but we shall get no more.

If here to-day the cloud of thunder lours
   To-morrow it will hie on far behests;
The flesh will grieve on other bones than ours
   Soon, and the soul will mourn in other breasts.

The troubles of our proud and angry dust
    Are from eternity, and shall not fail.
Bear them we can, and if we can we must.
    Shoulder the sky, my lad, and drink your ale.

Could man be drunk for ever
  With liquor, love, or fights,
Lief should I rouse at morning
  And lief lie down of nights.

But men at whiles are sober
  And think by fits and starts,
And if they think, they fasten
  Their hands upon their hearts.

Yonder see the morning blink:
   The sun is up, and up must I,
To wash and dress and eat and drink
And look at things and talk and think
   And work, and God knows why.

Oh often have I washed and dressed
   And what's to show for all my pain?
Let me lie abed and rest:
Ten thousand times I've done my best
   And all's to do again.

The laws of God, the laws of man,
He may keep that will and can;
Not I: let God and man decree
Laws for themselves and not for me;
And if my ways are not as theirs
Let them mind their own affairs.
Their deeds I judge and much condemn,
Yet when did I make laws for them?
Please yourselves, say I, and they
Need only look the other way.
But no, they will not; they must still
Wrest their neighbour to their will,
And make me dance as they desire
With jail and gallows and hell-fire.
And how am I to face the odds
Of man's bedevilment and God's?
I, a stranger and afraid
In a world I never made.
They will be master, right or wrong;
Though both are foolish, both are strong.
And since, my soul, we cannot fly
To Saturn nor to Mercury,
Keep we must, if keep we can,
These foreign laws of God and man.

THE DESERTER

'What sound awakened me, I wonder,
    For now 'tis dumb.'
'Wheels on the road most like, or thunder:
    Lie down; 'twas not the drum.'

Toil at sea and two in haven
    And trouble far:
Fly, crow, away, and follow, raven,
    And all that croaks for war.

'Hark, I heard the bugle crying,
    And where am I?
My friends are up and dressed and dying,
    And I will dress and die.'

'Oh love is rare and trouble plenty
    And carrion cheap,
And daylight dear at four-and-twenty:
    Lie down again and sleep.'

'Reach me my belt and leave your prattle:
    Your hour is gone;
But my day is the day of battle,
    And that comes dawning on.

'They mow the field of man in season:
    Farewell, my fair,
And, call it truth or call it treason,
    Farewell the vows that were.'

'Ay, false heart, forsake me lightly:
    'Tis like the brave.
They find no bed to joy in rightly
    Before they find the grave.

'Their love is for their own undoing,
    And east and west
They scour about the world a-wooing
    The bullet to their breast.

'Sail away the ocean over,
    Oh sail away,
And lie there with your leaden lover
    For ever and a day.'

THE CULPRIT

The night my father got me
  His mind was not on me;
He did not plague his fancy
  To muse if I should be
  The son you see.

The day my mother bore me
  She was a fool and glad,
For all the pain I cost her,
  That she had borne the lad
  That borne she had.

My mother and my father
  Out of the light they lie;
The warrant would not find them,
  And here 'tis only I
  Shall hang so high.

Oh let not man remember
  The soul that God forgot,
But fetch the county kerchief
  And noose me in the knot,
  And I will rot.

For so the game is ended
   That should not have begun.
My father and my mother
   They had a likely son,
   And I have none.

EIGHT O'CLOCK

He stood, and heard the steeple
  Sprinkle the quarters on the morning town.
One, two, three, four, to market-place and people
  It tossed them down.

Strapped, noosed, nighing his hour,
  He stood and counted them and cursed his luck;
And then the clock collected in the tower
  Its strength, and struck.

SPRING MORNING

Star and coronal and bell
    April underfoot renews,
And the hope of man as well
    Flowers among the morning dews.

Now the old come out to look,
    Winter past and winter's pains,
How the sky in pool and brook
    Glitters on the grassy plains.

Easily the gentle air
    Wafts the turning season on;
Things to comfort them are there,
    Though 'tis true the best are gone.

Now the scorned unlucky lad
    Rousing from his pillow gnawn
Mans his heart and deep and glad
    Drinks the valiant air of dawn.

Half the night he longed to die,
    Now are sown on hill and plain
Pleasures worth his while to try
    Ere he longs to die again.

Blue the sky from east to west
  Arches, and the world is wide,
Though the girl he loves the best
  Rouses from another's side.

ASTRONOMY

The Wain upon the northern steep
    Descends and lifts away.
Oh I will sit me down and weep
    For bones in Africa.

For pay and medals, name and rank,
    Things that he has not found,
He hove the Cross to heaven and sank
    The pole-star underground.

And now he does not even see
    Signs of the nadir roll
At night over the ground where he
    Is buried with the pole.

The rain, it streams on stone and hillock,
  The boot clings to the clay.
Since all is done that's due and right
Let's home; and now, my lad, good-night,
  For I must turn away.

Good-night, my lad, for nought's eternal;
  No league of ours, for sure.
To-morrow I shall miss you less,
And ache of heart and heaviness
  Are things that time should cure.

Over the hill the highway marches
  And what's beyond is wide:
Oh soon enough will pine to nought
Remembrance and the faithful thought
  That sits the grave beside.

The skies, they are not always raining
  Nor grey the twelvemonth through;
And I shall meet good days and mirth,
And range the lovely lands of earth
  With friends no worse than you.

But oh, my man, the house is fallen
  That none can build again;
My man, how full of joy and woe
Your mother bore you years ago
  To-night to lie in the rain.

In midnights of November,
    When Dead Man's Fair is nigh,
And danger in the valley,
    And anger in the sky,

Around the huddling homesteads
    The leafless timber roars,
And the dead call the dying
    And finger at the doors.

Oh, yonder faltering fingers
    Are hands I used to hold;
Their false companion drowses
    And leaves them in the cold.

Oh, to the bed of ocean,
    To Africk and to Ind,
I will arise and follow
    Along the rainy wind.

The night goes out and under
    With all its train forlorn;
Hues in the east assemble
    And cocks crow up the morn.

The living are the living
    And dead the dead will stay,
And I will sort with comrades
    That face the beam of day.

The night is freezing fast,
  To-morrow comes December;
    And winterfalls of old
Are with me from the past;
  And chiefly I remember
    How Dick would hate the cold.

Fall, winter, fall; for he,
  Prompt hand and headpiece clever,
    Has woven a winter robe,
And made of earth and sea
  His overcoat for ever,
    And wears the turning globe.

The fairies break their dances
    And leave the printed lawn,
And up from India glances
    The silver sail of dawn.

The candles burn their sockets,
    The blinds let through the day,
The young man feels his pockets
    And wonders what's to pay.

63

The half-moon westers low, my love,
   And the wind brings up the rain;
And wide apart lie we, my love,
   And seas between the twain.

I know not if it rains, my love,
   In the land where you do lie;
And oh, so sound you sleep, my love,
   You know no more than I.

64

The sigh that heaves the grasses
  Whence thou wilt never rise
Is of the air that passes
  And knows not if it sighs.

The diamond tears adorning
  Thy low mound on the lea,
Those are the tears of morning,
  That weeps, but not for thee.

65

Wake not for the world-heard thunder
   Nor the chime that earthquakes toll.
Star may plot in heaven with planet,
Lightning rive the rock of granite,
Tempest tread the oakwood under:
   Fear not you for flesh nor soul.
Marching, fighting, victory past,
Stretch your limbs in peace at last.

Stir not for the soldiers drilling
   Nor the fever nothing cures:
Throb of drum and timbal's rattle
Call but man alive to battle,
And the fife with death-notes filling
   Screams for blood but not for yours.
Times enough you bled your best;
Sleep on now, and take your rest.

Sleep, my lad; the French are landed,
   London's burning, Windsor's down;
Clasp your cloak of earth about you,
We must man the ditch without you,
March unled and fight short-handed,
   Charge to fall and swim to drown.
Duty, friendship, bravery o'er,
Sleep away, lad; wake no more.

66

SINNER'S RUE

I walked alone and thinking,
  And faint the nightwind blew
And stirred on mounds at crossways
  The flower of sinner's rue.

Where the roads part they bury
  Him that his own hand slays,
And so the weed of sorrow
  Springs at the four cross ways.

By night I plucked it hueless,
  When morning broke 'twas blue:
Blue at my breast I fastened
  The flower of sinner's rue.

It seemed a herb of healing,
  A balsam and a sign,
Flower of a heart whose trouble
  Must have been worse than mine.

Dead clay that did me kindness,
  I can do none to you,
But only wear for breastknot
  The flower of sinner's rue.

67

When I would muse in boyhood
  The wild green woods among,
And nurse resolves and fancies
  Because the world was young,
It was not foes to conquer,
  Nor sweethearts to be kind,
But it was friends to die for
  That I would seek and find.

I sought them far and found them,
  The sure, the straight, the brave,
The hearts I lost my own to,
  The souls I could not save.
They braced their belts about them,
  They crossed in ships the sea,
They sought and found six feet of ground,
  And there they died for me.

When the eye of day is shut,
  And the stars deny their beams,
And about the forest hut
  Blows the roaring wood of dreams,

From deep clay, from desert rock,
  From the sunk sands of the main,
Come not at my door to knock,
  Hearts that loved me not again.

Sleep, be still, turn to your rest
  In the lands where you are laid;
In far lodgings east and west
  Lie down on the beds you made.

In gross marl, in blowing dust,
  In the drowned ooze of the sea,
Where you would not, lie you must,
  Lie you must, and not with me.

THE FIRST OF MAY

The orchards half the way
   From home to Ludlow fair
Flowered on the first of May
   In Mays when I was there;
And seen from stile or turning
   The plume of smoke would show
Where fires were burning
   That went out long ago.

The plum broke forth in green,
   The pear stood high and snowed,
My friends and I between
   Would take the Ludlow road;
Dressed to the nines and drinking
   And light in heart and limb,
And each chap thinking
   The fair was held for him.

Between the trees in flower
   New friends at fairtime tread
The way where Ludlow tower
   Stands planted on the dead.
Our thoughts, a long while after,
   They think, our words they say;
Theirs now's the laughter,
   The fair, the first of May.

Ay, yonder lads are yet
    The fools that we were then;
For oh, the sons we get
    Are still the sons of men.
The sumless tale of sorrow
    Is all unrolled in vain:
May comes to-morrow
    And Ludlow fair again.

When first my way to fair I took
    Few pence in purse had I,
And long I used to stand and look
    At things I could not buy.

Now times are altered: if I care
    To buy a thing, I can;
The pence are here and here's the fair,
    But where's the lost young man?

—To think that two and two are four
    And neither five nor three
The heart of man has long been sore
    And long 'tis like to be.

REVOLUTION

West and away the wheels of darkness roll,
 Day's beamy banner up the east is borne,
Spectres and fears, the nightmare and her foal,
Drown in the golden deluge of the morn.

But over sea and continent from sight'
 Safe to the Indies has the earth conveyed
The vast and moon-eclipsing cone of night,
 Her towering foolscap of eternal shade.

See, in mid heaven the sun is mounted; hark,
 The belfries tingle to the noonday chime.
'Tis silent, and the subterranean dark
 Has crossed the nadir, and begins to climb.

EPITAPH ON AN ARMY OF MERCENARIES

These, in the day when heaven was falling,
  The hour when earth's foundations fled,
Followed their mercenary calling
  And took their wages and are dead.

Their shoulders held the sky suspended;
  They stood, and earth's foundations stay;
What God abandoned, these defended,
  And saved the sum of things for pay.

When summer's end is nighing
  And skies at evening cloud,
I muse on change and fortune
  And all the feats I vowed
  When I was young and proud.

The weathercock at sunset
  Would lose the slanted ray,
And I would climb the beacon
  That looked to Wales away
  And saw the last of day.

From hill and cloud and heaven
  The hues of evening died;
Night welled through lane and hollow
  And hushed the countryside,
  But I had youth and pride.

And I with earth and nightfall
  In converse high would stand,
Late, till the west was ashen
  And darkness hard at hand,
  And the eye lost the land.

The year might age, and cloudy
  The lessening day might close,
But air of other summers
  Breathed from beyond the snows,
  And I had hope of those.

They came and were and are not
   And come no more anew;
And all the years and seasons
   That ever can ensue
   Must now be worse and few.

So here's an end of roaming
   On eves when autumn nighs:
The ear too fondly listens
   For summer's parting sighs,
   And then the heart replies.

Tell me not here, it needs not saying,
  What tune the enchantress plays
In aftermaths of soft September
  Or under blanching mays,
For she and I were long acquainted
  And I knew all her ways.

On russet floors, by waters idle,
  The pine lets fall its cone;
The cuckoo shouts all day at nothing
  In leafy dells alone;
And traveller's joy beguiles in autumn
  Hearts that have lost their own.

On acres of the seeded grasses
  The changing burnish heaves;
Or marshalled under moons of harvest
  Stand still all night the sheaves;
Or beeches strip in storms for winter
  And stain the wind with leaves.

Possess, as I possessed a season,
  The countries I resign,
Where over elmy plains the highway
  Would mount the hills and shine,
And full of shade the pillared forest
Would murmur and be mine.

For nature, heartless, witless nature,
  Will neither care nor know
What stranger's feet may find the meadow
  And trespass there and go,
Nor ask amid the dews of morning
  If they are mine or no.

FANCY'S KNELL

When lads were home from labour
  At Abdon under Clee,
A man would call his neighbour
  And both would send for me.
And where the light in lances
  Across the mead was laid,
There to the dances
  I fetched my flute and played.

Ours were idle pleasures,
  Yet oh, content we were,
The young to wind the measures,
  The old to heed the air;
And I to lift with playing
  From tree and tower and steep
The light delaying,
  And flute the sun to sleep.

The youth toward his fancy
  Would turn his brow of tan,
And Tom would pair with Nancy
  And Dick step off with Fan;
The girl would lift her glances
  To his, and both be mute:
Well went the dances
  At evening to the flute.

Wenlock Edge was umbered,
   And bright was Abdon Burf,
And warm between them slumbered
   The smooth green miles of turf;
Until from grass and clover
   The upshot beam would fade,
And England over
   Advanced the lofty shade.

The lofty shade advances,
   I fetch my flute and play:
Come, lads, and learn the dances
   And praise the tune to-day.
To-morrow, more's the pity,
   Away we both must hie,
To air the ditty,
   And to earth I.

EASTER HYMN

If in that Syrian garden, ages slain,
You sleep, and know not you are dead in vain,
Nor even in dreams behold how dark and bright
Ascends in smoke and fire by day and night
The hate you died to quench and could but fan,
Sleep well and see no morning, son of man.

But if, the grave rent and the stone rolled by,
At the right hand of majesty on high
You sit, and sitting so remember yet
Your tears, your agony and bloody sweat,
Your cross and passion and the life you gave,
Bow hither out of heaven and see and save.

When Israel out of Egypt came
  Safe in the sea they trod;
By day in cloud, by night in flame,
  Went on before them God.

He brought them with a stretched out hand
  Dry-footed through the foam,
Past sword and famine, rock and sand,
  Lust and rebellion, home.

I never over Horeb heard
  The blast of advent blow;
No fire-faced prophet brought me word
  Which way behoved me go.

Ascended is the cloudy flame,
  The mount of thunder dumb;
The tokens that to Israel came,
  To me they have not come.

I see the country far away
  Where I shall never stand;
The heart goes where no footstep may
  Into the promised land.

The realm I look upon and die
  Another man will own;
He shall attain the heaven that I
  Perish and have not known.

But I will go where they are hid
   That never were begot,
To my inheritance amid
   The nation that is not.

For these of old the trader
  Unpearled the Indian seas,
The nations of the nadir
  Were diamondless for these;

A people prone and haggard
  Beheld their lightnings hurled:
All round, like Sinai, staggered
  The sceptre-shaken world.

But now their coins are tarnished,
  Their towers decayed away,
Their kingdom swept and garnished
  For haler kings than they;

Their arms the rust hath eaten,
  Their statutes none regard:
Arabia shall not sweeten
  Their dust, with all her nard.

They cease from long vexation,
  Their nights, their days are done,
The pale, the perished nation
  That never see the sun;

From the old deep-dusted annals
  The years erase their tale,
And round them race the channels
  That take no second sail.

79

THE SAGE TO THE YOUNG MAN

O youth whose heart is right,
  Whose loins are girt to gain
The hell-defended height
  Where Virtue beckons plain;

Who seest the stark array
  And hast not stayed to count
But singly wilt assay
  The many-cannoned mount:

Well is thy war begun;
  Endure, be strong and strive;
But think not, O my son,
  To save thy soul alive.

Wilt thou be true and just
  And clean and kind and brave?
Well; but for all thou dost,
  Be sure it shall not save.

Thou, when the night falls deep,
  Thou, though the mount be won,
High heart, thou shalt but sleep
  The sleep denied to none.

Others, or ever thou,
   To scale those heights were sworn;
And some achieved, but now
   They never see the morn.

How shouldst thou keep the prize?
   Thou wast not born for aye.
Content thee if thine eyes
   Behold it in thy day.

O youth that wilt attain,
   On, for thine hour is short.
It may be thou shalt gain
   The hell-defended fort.

DIFFUGERE NIVES

Horace: Odes iv 7

The snows are fled away, leaves on the shaws
   And grasses in the mead renew their birth,
The river to the river-bed withdraws,
   And altered is the fashion of the earth.

The Nymphs and Graces three put off their fear
   And unapparelled in the woodland play.
The swift hour and the brief prime of the year
   Say to the soul, *Thou wast not born for aye.*

Thaw follows frost; hard on the heel of spring
   Treads summer sure to die, for hard on hers
Comes autumn, with his apples scattering;
   Then back to wintertide, when nothing stirs.

But oh, whate'er the sky-led seasons mar,
   Moon upon moon rebuilds it with her beams:
Come *we* where Tullus and where Ancus are,
   And good Aeneas, we are dust and dreams.

Torquatus, if the gods in heaven shall add
   The morrow to the day, what tongue has told?
Feast then thy heart, for what thy heart has had
   The fingers of no heir will ever hold.

When thou descendest once the shades among,
  The stern assize and equal judgment o'er,
Not thy long lineage nor thy golden tongue,
  No, nor thy righteousness, shall friend thee more.

Night holds Hippolytus the pure of stain,
  Diana steads him nothing, he must stay;
And Theseus leaves Pirithöus in the chain
  The love of comrades cannot take away.

I to my perils
   Of cheat and charmer
   Came clad in armour
    By stars benign.
Hope lies to mortals
   And most believe her,
   But man's deceiver
    Was never mine.

The thoughts of others
   Were light and fleeting,
   Of lovers' meeting
    Or luck or fame.
Mine were of trouble,
   And mine were steady,
   So I was ready
    When trouble came.

When green buds hang in the elm like dust
  And sprinkle the lime like rain,
Forth I wander, forth I must,
  And drink of life again.
Forth I must by hedgerow bowers
  To look at the leaves uncurled,
And stand in fields where cuckoo-flowers
  Are lying about the world.

The weeping Pleiads wester,
  And the moon is under seas;
From bourn to bourn of midnight
  Far sighs the rainy breeze:

It sighs from a lost country
  To a land I have not known;
The weeping Pleiads wester,
  And I lie down alone.

84

I promise nothing: friends will part;
  All things may end, for all began;
And truth and singleness of heart
  Are mortal even as is man.

But this unlucky love should last
  When answered passions thin to air;
Eternal fate so deep has cast
  Its sure foundation of despair.

I lay me down and slumber
 And every morn revive.
Whose is the night-long breathing
 That keeps a man alive?

When I was off to dreamland
 And left my limbs forgot,
Who stayed at home to mind them,
 And breathed when I did not?

.   .   .   .

—I waste my time in talking,
 No heed at all takes he,
My kind and foolish comrade
 That breathes all night for me.

The farms of home lie lost in even,
　I see far off the steeple stand;
West and away from here to heaven
　Still is the land.

There if I go no girl will greet me,
　No comrade hollo from the hill,
No dog run down the yard to meet me:
　The land is still.

The land is still by farm and steeple,
　And still for me the land may stay:
There I was friends with perished people,
　And there lie they.

Tarry, delight, so seldom met,
  So sure to perish, tarry still;
Forbear to cease or languish yet,
  Though soon you must and will.

By Sestos town, in Hero's tower,
  On Hero's heart Leander lies;
The signal torch has burned its hour
  And sputters as it dies.

Beneath him, in the nighted firth,
  Between two continents complain
The seas he swam from earth to earth
  And he must swim again.

How clear, how lovely bright,
How beautiful to sight
    Those beams of morning play;
How heaven laughs out with glee
Where, like a bird set free,
Up from the eastern sea
    Soars the delightful day.

To-day I shall be strong,
No more shall yield to wrong,
    Shall squander life no more;
Days lost, I know not how,
I shall retrieve them now;
Now I shall keep the vow
    I never kept before.

Ensanguining the skies
How heavily it dies
    Into the west away;
Past touch and sight and sound,
Not further to be found,
How hopeless under ground
    Falls the remorseful day.

89

Ho, everyone that thirsteth
   And hath the price to give,
Come to the stolen waters,
   Drink and your soul shall live.

Come to the stolen waters,
   And leap the guarded pale,
And pull the flower in season
   Before desire shall fail.

It shall not last for ever,
   No more than earth and skies;
But he that drinks in season
   Shall live before he dies.

June suns, you cannot store them
   To warm the winter's cold,
The lad that hopes for heaven
   Shall fill his mouth with mould.

Crossing alone the nighted ferry
  With the one coin for fee,
Whom, on the wharf of Lethe waiting,
  Count you to find? Not me.

The brisk fond lackey to fetch and carry,
  The true, sick-hearted slave,
Expect him not in the just city
  And free land of the grave.

Good creatures, do you love your lives
   And have you ears for sense?
Here is a knife like other knives,
   That cost me eighteen pence.

I need but stick it in my heart
   And down will come the sky,
And earth's foundations will depart
   And all you folk will die.

On forelands high in heaven,
  'Tis many a year gone by,
Amidst the fall of even
  Would stand my friends and I.
Before our foolish faces
  Lay lands we did not see;
Our eyes were in the places
  Where we should never be.

'Oh, the pearl seas are yonder,
  The amber-sanded shore;
Shires where the girls are fonder,
  Towns where the pots hold more.
And here fret we and moulder
  By grange and rick and shed
And every moon are older,
  And soon we shall be dead.'

Heigho, 'twas true and pity;
  But there we lads must stay.
Troy was a steepled city,
  But Troy was far away.
And round we turned lamenting
  To homes we longed to leave,
And silent hills indenting
  The orange band of eve.

I see the air benighted
  And all the dusking dales,
And lamps in England lighted,
  And evening wrecked on Wales;
And starry darkness paces
  The road from sea to sea,
And blots the foolish faces
  Of my poor friends and me.

Young is the blood that yonder
    Strides out the dusty mile,
And breasts the hillside highway
    And whistles loud the while,
    And vaults the stile.

Yet flesh, now too, has thorn-pricks,
    And shoulders carry care,
Even as in other seasons,
    When I and not my heir
    Was young and there.

On miry meads in winter
    The football sprang and fell;
May stuck the land with wickets:
    For all the eye could tell,
    The world went well.

Yet well, God knows, it went not,
    God knows, it went awry;
For me, one flowery Maytime,
    It went so ill that I
    Designed to die.

And if so long I carry
    The lot that season marred,
'Tis that the sons of Adam
    Are not so evil-starred
    As they are hard.

Young is the blood that yonder
   Succeeds to rick and fold,
Fresh are the form and favour
   And new the minted mould:
   The thoughts are old.

94

Here dead lie we because we did not choose
  To live and shame the land from which we sprung.
Life, to be sure, is nothing much to lose;
  But young men think it is, and we were young.

By shores and woods and steeples
  Rejoicing hearts receive
Poured on a hundred peoples
  The far-shed alms of eve.

Her hands are filled with slumber
  For world-wide labourers worn;
Yet those are more in number
  That know her not from morn.

Now who sees night for ever,
  He sees no happier sight:
Night and no moon and never
  A star upon the night.

I wake from dreams and turning
    My vision on the height
I scan the beacons burning
    About the fields of night.

Each in its steadfast station
    Inflaming heaven they flare;
They sign with conflagration
    The empty moors of air.

The signal-fires of warning
    They blaze, but none regard;
And on through night to morning
    The world runs ruinward.

Smooth between sea and land
Is laid the yellow sand,
And here through summer days
The seed of Adam plays.

Here the child comes to found
His unremaining mound,
And the grown lad to score
Two names upon the shore.

Here, on the level sand,
Between the sea and land,
What shall I build or write
Against the fall of night?

Tell me of runes to grave
That hold the bursting wave,
Or bastions to design
For longer date than mine.

Shall it be Troy or Rome
I fence against the foam,
Or my own name, to stay
When I depart for aye?

Nothing: too near at hand,
Planing the figured sand,
Effacing clean and fast
Cities not built to last
And charms devised in vain,
Pours the confounding main.

FOR MY FUNERAL

O thou that from thy mansion,
  Through time and place to roam,
Dost send abroad thy children,
  And then dost call them home,

That men and tribes and nations
  And all thy hand hath made
May shelter them from sunshine
  In thine eternal shade:

We now to peace and darkness
  And earth and thee restore
Thy creature that thou madest
  And wilt cast forth no more.

PARTA QUIES

Good-night; ensured release,
Imperishable peace,
   Have these for yours,
While sea abides, and land,
And earth's foundations stand,
   And heaven endures.

When earth's foundations flee,
Nor sky nor land nor sea
   At all is found,
Content you, let them burn:
It is not your concern;
   Sleep on, sleep sound.

The stars have not dealt me the worst they could do:
My pleasures are plenty, my troubles are two.
But oh, my two troubles they reave me of rest,
The brains in my head and the heart in my breast.

Oh grant me the ease that is granted so free,
The birthright of multitudes, give it to me,
That relish their victuals and rest on their bed
With flint in the bosom and guts in the head.

Translation

Sophocles, *Oedipus Coloneus* (lines 1211–1248)

What man is he that yearneth
   For length unmeasured of days?
Folly mine eye discerneth
   Encompassing all his ways.
For years over-running the measure
   Shall change thee in evil wise:
Grief draweth nigh thee; and pleasure,
   Behold, it is hid from thine eyes.
   This to their wage have they
   Which overlive their day.
And He that looseth from labour
   Doth one with other befriend,
   Whom bride nor bridesmen attend,
Song, nor sound of the tabor,
   Death, that maketh an end.

Thy portion esteem I highest,
   Who wast not ever begot;
Thine next, being born who diest
   And straightway again art not.

With follies light as the feather
   Doth Youth to man befall;
Then evils gather together,
   There wants not one of them all—
   Wrath, envy, discord, strife,
   The sword that seeketh life.
And sealing the sum of trouble
   Doth tottering Age draw nigh,
   Whom friends and kinsfolk fly,
Age, upon whom redouble
   All sorrows under the sky.

This man, as me, even so,
Have the evil days overtaken;
And like as a cape sea-shaken
With tempest at earth's last verges
And shock of all winds that blow,
His head the seas of woe,
The thunders of awful surges
Ruining overflow;
Blown from the fall of even,
   Blown from the dayspring forth,
Blown from the noon in heaven,
   Blown from night and the North.

Notes on the Poems

Poems in this selection are given Arabic numerals; those not included but to which reference is made are given, as Housman gave them, Roman numerals, and are to be found in *The Collected Poems of A. E. Housman* (Jonathan Cape, 1971) from which the text of the poems included here is taken. Where Housman gave a poem a title, this is also given here, as it is in the text and the Index.

The following abbreviations are used: *ASL, A Shropshire Lad*, first published in 1896; *LP, Last Poems*, first published in 1922; *MP, More Poems* first published in 1936; *AP, Additional Poems* (the first 18 were published in Laurence Housman's *Memoir* of his brother in 1937, and another five were added in the Collected Poems of 1939).

Poems referred to in the Introduction and the Notes which are *not* in the Selection are asterisked.

The notebooks sometimes referred to in the Introduc-duction and the Notes are thus described by his brother Laurence:

'The four note-books containing the original drafts of the bulk of A.E.H.'s poems, and also a few fair copies in the actual form in which they were published, cannot all be definitely divided in date; and though I have made a guess and distinguished them by the letters A, B, C, and D, I cannot be sure that they came to be used in that order: except for A, which is certainly the first, since it contains three of the earliest poems (one dating as far back as 1890), and also more *Shropshire Lad* poems, and fewer *Last Poems* than any of the three others.'

It is from these notebooks that Laurence Housman selected the poems that make up *More Poems* and *Additional Poems*. In his brother's will he had been instructed to destroy all poems that were below a certain standard and any unfinished verses.

1. *ASL II.* One of the best-known and -loved poems of *ASL*.

2. *ASL III.* It is dated Jan. 1895 in Housman's notebooks.
   ASL opens with a poem (*I) on the Jubilee of the Queen (Victoria) in 1887, and celebrates the part played by her soldiers.
   lands of morn (l. 18): eastern countries.

3. *ASL IV.* The first draft of the poem is dated Jan. 1895 in the notebooks.
   In spite of the title and *the drums of morning*, the poem is not one of Housman's military poems but an exhortation to a life of energy and effort. The splendour of imagery and diction of the first two stanzas is in designed contrast with the simplicity and familiarity of the rest: the example of dawn is beautiful and stirring. The brisk and alert metre accords with the theme. *Straws* (l. 8) is dialectal and archaic for 'strews'.

4. *ASL V.* Probably written at the end of 1894 or in the first months of 1895. It is an account, cheerful in sentiment and metre, of a baffled attempt at seduction.

The innocence, as it were, of the piece is established by its references to posy-picking, buttercups (*goldcup* is a dialect word) and to the childish and rural custom of blowing away the 'clocks' or downy heads of dandelions to tell the time. The poem has something of the quality of the song in *As You Like It*—'It was a lover and his lass'.

ASL VI is an ironic and sad poem of the girl who yields.

5. *ASL VII.* Probably written August-September 1895. The first example of the five-line stanza that Housman invented, and used with such effect in, e.g., *Bredon Hill.*

6. *ASL VIII.* Dated Aug. 1894 in the notebooks. This, together with Nos. 18 and 27 of *ASL*, are tragic stories in the ballad manner, and are soaked with their sentiment and phraseology. A ballad which invites comparison is *Edward*, but parallels in thought and manner can be found in several.

The last stanza speaks of the familiar and homely about to be lost, as the dead men who are returning to their graves speak in one of the finest of the traditional ballads, *The Wife of Usher's Well*:

> Fare ye weel, my mother dear!
> Farewell to barn and byre!
> And fare ye weel, the bonny lass
> That kindles my mother's fire!

In a draft of the poem in the notebooks, a motive is supplied—the young men quarrelled about Lucy. But the best ballads do not usually supply motives, and neither does the final version of this.

Lammastide (l. 19): Lammas is the feast of first-fruits, August 1st.

7. *ASL IX*. First draft Feb. 1895.

l. 27. Eight was the legal time for executions. See No. 56, *Eight O'Clock*, and the terrible last few paragraphs of *Tess of the D'Urbervilles*.

8. *ASL X*. Perhaps written before the end of 1894. Like No. 3, this poem has a splendid couple of opening stanzas, here astrological, and, like it, passes into rural simplicities, the expeditions for palms and daffodils.

The Ram (l. 4) is the Ram of the Zodiac, Chrysomalion, whose golden fleece was stolen by Jason in his Argonautic expedition. It was transposed to the stars and made the first sign of the Zodiac. The Ram is the first of the spring signs. The *silver Pair* (l. 2) are the fishes (Pisces), the last of the winter signs. *To higher air* (l. 1): in passing from February to March (or from winter to spring), the sun mounts higher.

storm-cock (l. 5): missel-thrush.

palms (l. 13): branches of the silver willow, used especially for celebrating Palm Sunday in northern countries.

9. *ASL XII*. Probably written in the early months of 1895. It has a fairly strong Biblical flavour: e.g., ll. 5–6, 'the lusts of the flesh' (II *Peter*, 2.18); 'our earthly house' (II *Corinthians*, 5.1). l. 7 *house of dust*: 'death ... the house appointed for all living' (*Job* 30:23); 'Ye that dwell in the dust' (*Isaiah* 26:19).

10. *ASL XIII*. First draft dated Jan. 1895.

11. *ASL XIV*. The poem appears early in Housman's first
    notebook, and may belong to the late 1880's. Per-
    haps there is concealed autobiography here.
   sain (l..13): the word is archaic and dialectal. Housman
obviously takes it to be from Latin *sanare* 'to cure', 'heal',
but it is in fact an Anglo-Saxon borrowing from Latin
signare 'to sign with the cross', hence 'to bless'.

12. *ASL XVI*. This economical little masterpiece is not per-
    haps as simple as it seems, and is capable of mis-
    interpretation. The lover of the second stanza is in
    apposition to the lovers of the first: they committed
    suicide for frustrated love, he for love of the grave,
    i.e. because he was out of love with life. But the last
    two lines are designedly ambiguous: they could also
    imply that he loved the grave because human love
    failed him.
   The dancing nettle is a sour symbol. It appears in *MP
XXXII* as a symbol of flourishing harm and ill. One ex-
pects beautiful flowers, like Wordsworth's daffodils, to
dance; the dance of the nettle is ironic, and suggests
malicious glee.
   recovers (l. 1) is a term from dancing: 'rises again after
bowing or curtseying'.

13. *ASL XIX*. Probably belongs to the opening months of
    1895. The theme of this splendid sombre poem is as
    if one of Pindar's odes celebrating athletic victories
    at the various Greek festivals had married such a
    chorus from Greek tragedy as that which Housman

chose to translate from Sophocles' *Œdipus Coloneus* (p. 181), about the benefit of early death.

The world and state of the dead is always pagan in Housman, as it is here in the last two stanzas. Homer described the dead as *amenēna karēna*, figures without vital strength, and bloodless. *Strengthless* (l. 26) here is moving and ironic in relation to a young athlete.

The world of classical reference mingles with the homely setting and familiar tone of *Smart lad* (l. 9) and *lads* (l. 18).

The MS of the poem indicates hard work before the final perfection was reached. *Cannot see the record cut* (l. 14) had to be explained by Housman to an admirer. The original reading of the lines, though feeble and partly meaningless, was

> Eyes the night has filled with smoke
> Never see the record broke

which makes the meaning of *cut* clear—'reduce the recorded shortest time for a race'.

14. *ASL XX.* Probably mid-1895.

15. *ASL XXI.* The first draft of this poem is dated by Housman July 1891. It is one of the most popular poems of *ASL*, and has attracted composers. The simple language, and, in part, the theme, are ballad-like, but the pattern of the stanza is Housman's own invention, and is used in seven other poems. The metrical secret of the pattern is in the last line, which successively confirms, extends, destroys and succumbs.

It is the earliest of the poems with place-names, but it was written before Housman had conceived of a Shropshire cycle. Bredon Hill is in Worcestershire.

coloured counties (l. 8): Worcestershire, Gloucestershire, Herefordshire, Warwickshire. To the west and north are the Welsh mountains.

16. *ASL XXIII.* The metre—fourteeners— is not common in Housman, and he is not at his best in it, though the last two lines are splendid.

   till (l. 5): tillage, ploughing.

17. *ASL XXVI.* June (? 1895).

18. *ASL XXVII.* This fine poem is probably the nearest, as a whole, that Housman came to the traditional ballad in form and feeling. The poem is entirely in dialogue of great dramatic strength like *Edward*; the 'ghost' is the 'living' dead man of ballad conception. Ghosts come back in the ballad for various reasons, sometimes because of the tears of the living, sometimes, as here, because there is nothing in the grave, and nothing more desirable than earthly pursuits—in this poem football and ploughing—and earthly love. The revenant here is pathetically anxious about his girl; his false friend grows progressively more uneasy until the bitter and ironical end. The most touching of all dead visitations in the traditional ballad is in *Sweet William's Ghost*, where the lovers are true.

This poem was Hardy's favourite, perhaps because of its tragic irony, and was set to music by Vaughan Williams.

19 *ASL XXVIII*. Dated in the notebook Jan. 1895. A poem of internal conflict externalised in the Saxon conquest of the Welsh. The imagery of stanza 2 is superb.

The situation imagined is that of the Anglo-Saxon conquest of Shrewsbury from the Welsh. In 779, Offa, King of Mercia, pushed across the Severn and drove the Welsh King of Powys from the town. He later consolidated his gains in Shropshire by building defensive earthworks, now known as Offa's Dyke, against the Welsh.

Buildwas (l. 13): a small place on the Severn, above Coalbrookdale, a few miles south-east of Shrewsbury, and later (1135) the site of a Cistercian abbey.

Housman originally wrote *Bewdley*, a town in Shropshire lower down the Severn.

20. *ASL XXIX*. Dated in the notebook April 1895.

Lenten lily (l. 8): daffodil. In folklore, the daffodil dies on Easter Day.

windflower (l. 13): a poetical name for the wood-anemone; *anemone* means 'windflower' in Greek.

21. *ASL XXX*. Written probably in the first five months of 1895.

Housman, who thought very highly of Arnold, may have remembered his statement of his unsatisfactory love in *Destiny*:

> They
> [i.e. 'the Powers that sport with man']
> Yoked in him for endless strife
> A heart of ice, a soul of fire;
> And hurled him on the Field of Life,
> An aimless unallayed Desire.

22. *ASL XXXI.* The first draft is dated in the notebook
 Nov. 1895. The theme, beautifully expressed in terms
 of nature as well as the heart of man, is the perma-
 nence and persistence of trouble, only to be ended
 by death. The poem is partly written in the style of
 the supposed speaker, 'an English yeoman'.

Wenlock Edge (l. 1): South of Shrewsbury and south of the
Severn; a level hill which stretches from Craven Arms to
Much Wenlock.

the Wrekin (l. 2): a hill of nearly 1,350 feet, quite
wild and impressive, north of the Severn and east of
Shrewsbury.

holt (l. 5): a wood or copse. Now poetical and dialectal,
but found in many place-names.

hanger (l. 5): a wood on the side of a steep hill or bank;
the word is also now found in place-names.

Uricon (l. 6): Uriconium, Viroconium; modern Wrox-
eter, near Shrewsbury, where the Romans built a legionary
fortress as a base for their campaigns against the Welsh
tribes in the first century A.D.

23. *ASL XXXII.* Perhaps before the end of 1894. Perhaps
 here, as some think, Housman has Lucretius's atom-
 istic theory of life in mind. In this there is the com-
 ing together of first particles (*concilium*) to make the
 compound, man; then, at death, the dissolution of
 things into their component atoms (*discidium*).
 endless way (l. 12) may be explained (perhaps) in
 Lucretian terms:

solidissima materiai

corpora perpetuo volitare invicta per aevum

—the most solid bodies of matter fly about for ever

unvanquished through the ages.

(*De Rerum Natura*, III, 951–2)

Death, to Lucretius, only scatters the union of atoms. He more than once speaks of the soul at death as scattering into air (*disceḍit in auras*, *D.R.N.* III, 400).

Man is seen against this background in the poem.

twelve-winded (l. 2): Homer knew only four winds, but Aristotle produced twelve, coming from the twelve parts of the earth (l. 11).

23. *ASL XXXIII*. Perhaps before the end of 1894.

25. *ASL XXXV*. See Introduction, pp. 22–3.

food for powder (l. 7).

Housman ironically uses Falstaff's contemptuous description of his wretched recruits for the Battle of Shrewsbury.

See *Henry IV*, Part I, Act IV, Scene II—

Prince . . . But tell me, Jack, whose fellows are these that come after?

Falstaff Mine, Hal, mine.

Prince I did never see such pitiful rascals.

Falstaff Tut, tut; good enough to toss; food for powder, food for powder; they'll fill a pit as well as better: tush, man, mortal men, mortal men.

Compare *Epitaph on an Army of Mercenaries* (No. 72) for a sustained example of the same kind of irony.

26. *ASL XXXVI*. One of the most beautiful of the love-lyrics.

blank (l. 2) may have its current meaning or its etymological meaning ('white'), or both.

27. *ASL XXXVII*. Perhaps August or September 1895.

28. *ASL XXXVIII*. Perhaps also August or September 1895.

29. *ASL XXXIX*. Dated by Housman in the notebook Feb. 1893.

30. *ASL XL*. Occurs at the beginning of Notebook A as a fair copy, slightly corrected. It is the first *Shropshire Lad* poem in the book. This suggests a very early date. It is one of the most poignant lyrics of longing that he ever wrote.

31. *ASL XLI*. The first draft of this is dated Nov. 1895 in the notebooks.

32. *ASL XLII*. This is dated Sept. 1890 in Notebook A, and is therefore, probably, the earliest poem in the *Shropshire Lad*. It is the second longest of Housman's poems. *Hell Gate (*LP XXXI)* is the longest, with 104 lines.

The Merry Guide is Hermes, the Greek god who was charged with guiding travellers on their dangerous ways, and also with conducting the souls of the dead to the Underworld. He was represented as wearing a feathered cap and feathered sandals, which symbolised his speed, and, as messenger of the gods, he carried a golden rod, the caduceus, usually shown with two serpents twined round it. In his character as conductor of souls, he was known as Hermes Psychopompos. In Hesiod he brings to men's hearts the sentiments and impressions that Zeus has inspired.

In this poem, his looks promise delight and merriment on life's journey, but he says nothing of its purpose and end; and all that dies in nature travels onward with him and man.

In this lovely lyric, rich in felicitous compound epithets, the delight of youth, hope and nature is in the foreground, but it is clear enough that life's questions are not to be answered, and that the journey is with lost blossoms and bereaved woods, and 'the fluttering legion of all that ever died'.

33. *ASL XLIII*. Probably early in 1895—at least as a first draft.

The title is ironical: the 'immortal part' is the skeleton, which, in the thought of the poem, is contemptuous of the body it bears, and the schemes and dreams of the mind. The poem is entirely materialistic, and might have been written by a lover of Lucretius; and this is true even of the penultimate stanza, where the will is asserted; for Lucretius says:

> *tamen esse in pectore nostro*
> *quiddam quod contra pugnare obstareque possit*

—yet there is something in our breast which can fight against it and withstand it.

By the 'it' of the translation, Lucretius means both an outside force and the 'will' of the body. l. 30 is an echo of the first line of the song in *Cymbeline*, 'Fear no more the heat o' th' sun', which Housman in *The Name and Nature of Poetry* spoke of as among 'those songs, the very summits of lyrical achievement'.

ancient night (l. 43): epithets referring to the antiquity of

Night ('the ancestress of gods and men') are drawn from the classics. cf. Milton, *Paradise Lost*, II, 962—'Sable-vested Night, eldest of things.'

34. *ASL XLVII*. Dated in Notebook B, August 1895. A deeply ironical poem, where the speaker (a thinly disguised Christ) is seen to be hanged for love. The verses express a deep sense of the futility of the Sacrifice on the Cross, but sympathy for the sufferer, and contempt for the world which rejects him.
    See No. 76.

35. *ASL XLVIII*. On the evidence of the notebooks, this seems to have been composed in 1892 or 1893.
    the quarry (l. 5): the shapeless material from which human life comes.
    The last stanza might be compared with Lucretius:

>   *ne quaquam nobis divinitus esse paratam*
>   *naturam rerum: tanta stat praedita culpa.*

—By no means has the nature of things been fashioned for us by divine grace: so great are the flaws with which it stands beset.   (*D.R.N.* V, 198–9, trs. Cyril Bailey)

36. *ASL L*. The italicised quatrain is not Housman's, but traditional, and tradition has less complimentary names as variations for 'quietest', such as 'sleepiest', 'drunkenest', 'dirtiest', and worse. Housman added the verse in proof.
    Ony, Teme, Clun (l. 2): little Shropshire rivers.
    handselled (l. 16): an obsolete and dialect word, probably meaning here 'used for the first time' (said e.g. of a plough).

37. *ASL LII*. Dated in the notebook 1891–2, and therefore one of the earliest poems of the *Shropshire Lad*.

weirs (l. 16): pools (an obsolete sense except in dialect).

38. *ASL LIII*. First draft Dec. 1894.

The title is at least semi-ironic. Some dislike the poem because of alleged tastelessness. It has the authentic ballad theme and tone.

39. *ASL LIV*. Dated in the Notebook Aug. 1893.

This exquisite lyric seems to have been a favourite poem for schoolboys to turn into Latin or Greek. Its formal beauty explains its choice for this purpose. It is very like some poems of Heine in its brevity and tone.

golden (l. 2), may have been influenced by one of Housman's favourite poems, the Dirge in *Cymbeline*, where Shakespeare speaks of 'golden lads and girls' who must come to dust; but it is classical also: Horace (*Odes*, I, 5) calls Pyrrha a 'golden maid'.

40. *ASL LV*. This seems to belong to early 1895.

l. 14 cf. Milton, *Comus*, l. 139, 'The nice Morn on the Indian steep', where *steep* means 'sky'.

41. *ASL LIX*. A draft of this is found in Notebook A, so that it is an early poem.

Portland Prison is on the Isle of Portland, off the coast of Dorset. The poem is one of several on young men who are executed.

42. *ASL LXI*. Probably before the end of 1894. See Introduction, p. 9.

43. *ASL LXII.* This appears in draft in Notebook A, and
    apparently belongs to the second half of 1894.

The poem has some of the best-known lines of Hous-
man. The poet (Terence) here appears as a member of the
rural community and speaks as one, with rustic humour
and phraseology. In the third stanza, the bucolic Terence
turns into the poet Housman, with some impressive lines.
The poem shows, like some others, that Housman can
laugh at his own melancholy.

The reference in stanza one is to the phrase 'the tune
the cow died of', the subject of a comic song. An old man
who had an old cow, but had no fodder to give her, played
and sang to her on his fiddle:

> Consider, good cow, consider,
> This isn't the time for the grass to grow:
> Consider, good cow, consider.

The phrase refers therefore to the offering of advice or
remonstrance instead of help. It means also bad verses.

Mithridates VI, King of Pontus and Bithynia, in the first
century B.C. made himself immune from poison by gradu-
ally increasing doses. He was killed at the hands of a guard
at the age of sixty-eight.

44. *ASL LXIII.* This is the last poem of *A Shropshire Lad*, and
    appropriately so, since by the neglected flowers he
    seems to imply his poems, with a deprecatory
    anticipation.

The page containing this poem is missing in the note-
book, no doubt to prevent anyone knowing whether or
not he had solved the riddle propounded in *The Name and*

Nature of Poetry. In this lecture Housman reveals his methods of composing—beer, a long walk, inspiration. One of the four stanzas would not come. 'I wrote it thirteen times, and it was more than a twelvemonth before I got it right.' He would never divulge which this was.

45. *LP I*. Housman dated this about 1905. Though the general meaning of the poem is clear, some details are not.

Housman from boyhood was fascinated by the West. The *forty counties* (l. 10) seem to be the counties of England which lie at his back as he gazes over Wales at the sunset. This is the physical stance of the poem.

But the West also appears to be the spiritual home of the speaker, beguiling him to leave his clothes upon the sands, and drown in the western sea. In this sense, it is death and its allurements. It is the speaker's *native land* (stanza 10) but it must not be sought too soon.

There is apparently a change of metaphor between stanza 7 and the last stanza: in the former, the speaker is thinking of the sea of matter out of which he and his friend were made, and to which they must return; in the latter there is what appears to be a Lucretian phrase, *spilt on air*, which, far from suggesting drowning in matter, implies the diffusion of the body into its atoms.

46. *LP II*. This was published in *The Blunderbuss*, a Trinity College, Cambridge, magazine, in March 1917.

47. *LP III*. Dated by Housman 1895.

This mysterious, attractive poem would appear to be an allegory. One of Housman's nephews, Lt. C. A. Symons, copied it into his autograph book shortly before he was killed at Loos in autumn 1915, thinking it expressed the conquest of fear; and in *Last Poems* it is followed by the poem *Illic Jacet* which Housman wrote for his death, and sent to his mother. It was first published in *The Edwardian*, the magazine of King Edward's School at Bath in December 1915 under the title of *The Conflict*. It was intended for *ASL*, but cancelled in page-proof.

limbecks (l. 3): 'limbeck' is a contracted form, now obsolete, of 'alembic'—a glass flask used by chemists.

The Queen of air and darkness (l. 5) seems to be Hecate, who in Greek mythology was Goddess of Night, of goblins, of magic and the Underworld, as well as of the Moon. Attacks of fear and terror at night were thought to be due to her assaults. The poem shows that her bogeys can be overcome by resolution, and are, as it were, airy nothings.

48. *LP VII*. Written in April 1922; but the last verse was 'written long previously'.

49. *LP VIII*. This was written mainly in 1905. It seems most unlikely that it should have anything but the remotest reference to the death of his youngest brother, Herbert, in South Africa on 30 October 1901, though this has been suggested. Soldiers are simply closest to death in Housman; and soldiers who escape it in war wait for it in the human *inn of night*. There is deadly surprise in the last two lines.

Kesar (l. 12) is an archaic form of 'Kaiser'; 'Kings and Kesars', a common Middle English alliterative phrase, in modern use is an archaism, revived mainly by Scott.

Housman uses this to distance or make timeless the in-evitable lot of man.

50. *LP IX*. Most of this was written in February 1896, but the last sombre verse was written in April 1922, no doubt to point the moral. Critics tend to miss the wry humour, even at the expense of his own philosophy, in Housman. The curses here are pub curses which most of us have uttered, without necessarily sub-scribing to a grand general philosophy, such as that of the last stanza. The poem is a masterpiece of high and low sentiment and expression. In some sense, Housman is the poet of eager and expectant youth —'of effort, expectation and desire' in Wordsworth's phrase.

hie on far behests (l. 22): 'hasten off on other duties far away'. Implicit in the phrase, as indeed in the whole poem, is the notion of either a malignant or an indifferent fate. *behests* means 'commands'.

51. *LP X*. Written some time between 1900 and 1905.

52. *LP XI*. Dated Dec. 1895. A kind of comedy of boredom and routine.

53. *LP XII*. Written about 1900.

54. *LP XIII*. Begun 1905; finished April 1922. Housman said it was set to the tune of a shanty heard at Hereford.

The title is ironical, as so often in Housman. It is the girl who is deserted, not the Army. The poem is cast in the form of a dialogue between a lover and his girl in bed, except for stanza 2, which is a kind of ballad chorus.

The situation here is like that of the ballad, *The Braes of Yarrow*; and the ravens croak for war in *The Twa Corbies*. The use of dialogue almost throughout is also ballad-like.

The poem might be compared with Auden's poem VI in *Look, Stranger!*—'O what is that sound that so thrills the ear?'; and again, with Wilfred Owen's bitter, ironic poem, *Greater Love*—'Red lips are not so red'; and the girl's lament in Housman's poem here, that her love is rejected for that of the bullet, with Owen's

> these blind, blunt bullet-leads
> which long to nuzzle in the hearts of lads
> *(Arms and the Boy)*

55. *LP XIV*. Dated by Housman before 1910.
county kerchief (l. 18): hangman's noose.

56. *LP XV*. Written in 1921.
One of the most brilliant examples of Housman's lapidary art. The focus is on the clock, on which so much of this art is spent, that the victim might, at first sight, seem neglected. But *his* interest is in the clock, too, and he awaits with painful concentration the transition from the lightness of 'sprinkle' and the indifference of 'tossed', to the massive blow of the second stanza.
Tossed was reached after eight rejections—'loosed', 'spilt', 'cast', 'told', 'dealt', 'pitched', 'dropped', 'flung'.

57. *LP XVI*. Begun 1900, finished 1922.

58. *LP XVII*. Housman says it was written before 1904. It occurs on the last few pages of Notebook B, which

were written during the Boer War (October 1899–May 1902). Housman's youngest brother, Herbert, was killed there on 30 October 1901. First printed in *Wayfarer's Love: Contributions from Living Poets* (1904).

The original title, *The Use of the Globes*, was more clearly ironical than the title Housman finally gave it. The use of the globes (i.e. the terrestrial and celestial globes) was taught in schools, and was the expected equipment of every governess and teacher. With this title, the ostensible theme of the poem would be a school-subject.

Wain (l. 1): the group of seven bright stars in the northern sky about the North Pole; the constellation called the Great Bear.

steep (l. 1): a poetical word for sky.

Cross (l. 7): the Southern Cross, a striking constellation of the Southern hemisphere: the soldier in journeying to South Africa saw instead of the familiar Pole Star of the Northern hemisphere, the Southern Cross; fancifully, the Pole Star is under his feet, and he is thought of as being buried with it.

Signs of the nadir (l. 10): are those constellations which are seen in South Africa, i.e., as it were, below the feet of the observer in England.

59, *LP XVIII*. Begun 1902, finished 1922.

60. *LP XIX*. Begun 1895, finished 1905. This has a good deal of the eerie atmosphere of a supernatural ballad. Midnight, the roaring trees, the dead fingering the doors, and the fearful name of the fair have a powerful effect. Housman took the name of the fair from folk tradition. *Dead Man's Fair* was the

name, now obsolete, of the fair held at Church Stretton in Shropshire on St Andrew's Day (2 December). 'It acquired this ominous name from the circumstance, it is said, of the number of men, who in attempting to cross the hills on their return home after attending the fair, lost their way and perished.' (Wright, *English Dialect Dictionary*.)

As mentioned in the Introduction, Housman acknowledged only three literary influences on his poetry—the songs of Shakespeare, ballads, and Heine. There is one of the clear instances of a borrowing from Heine in lines 21–2. Heine writes in *Die Ilse*

> *Es bleiben tot die Toten*
> *Und nur der Lebendige lebt*

—the dead stay dead, and only the living man lives.

The poem gave Housman much trouble before he arrived at the felicity we know; e.g. the dead first *whistled* at the doors, and the pathetic *faltering* (l. 9) was originally 'frozen'.

sort (l. 23): associate with.

61. *LP XX*. Written April 1922.

This clever but tender poem prevents any possible sentimentality by the wry humour of its conceit. The ironic proof of Dick's cleverness is that he has stolen a march on winter by wearing the globe itself. Moreover, the poem is clever as well as Dick. Housman was by no means averse from conceits. This one has been compared with those of Donne and the metaphysicals, but actually it is more visual and more Elizabethan than theirs usually are. The notion of wearing the earth as a cloak is found not only in Greek and Latin poetry, but even, in a simple way, in the ballad. The last stanza of *The Gardener* has

> 'The new-fallen snow to be your smock;
> Becomes your body neat;
> And your head shall be decked with the
>   eastern wind,
> And the cold rain on your breast.'

The prosaic *overcoat* of line II is a stroke of genius in the context, for it brings into conjunction the familiar needs and habits of men and their mighty, impersonal environment. The last great stanza of *The Wife of Usher's Well* has this same homeliness, but not its vastness.

62. *LP XXI*. Written between 1900 and 1905.

This is a fine example of formal parallelism, with tonal and phrasal opposition between the first and second stanzas.

The next two poems *XXII* and *XXIII* have something of the same quality.

63. *LP XXVI*. Written April 1922.

Compare the opening stanza of the ballad *The Unquiet Grave*:

> The wind doth blow today, my love,
>   And a few small drops of rain;
> I never had but one true-love,
>   In cold grave she was lain.

64. *LP XXVII*. Written soon after 1900.

65. *LP XXIX.* Dated 30 March 1922.

rive (l.4): split (now rare or unknown in Standard English).

timbal (l.11): (now historical) Kettle-drum.

the French are landed etc. (l.25): imaginary military disastors, to which the dead soldier can now be indifferent.

66. *LP XXX.* Written between 1910 and 1922.

The poem is an expansion and adaptation of Heine's *Am Kreuzweg wird begraben*, a poem which, literally translated, is:

'The man who killed himself is buried at the cross-roads; a blue flower grows there, the poor sinner's flower.

'I stood at the cross-roads and sighed; the night was cold and silent. In the moonshine, the poor sinner's flower waved slowly to and fro.'

Housman keeps the metre and rhyme-scheme of the original, and ends every second stanza with the name of the flower. Each of Heine's two stanzas end with *Die Armesünderblum'* (literally 'the poor wretch's flower') as a single line. This is a German country name for the blue flower of the wild chicory.

Housman originally gave the poem the title *Die Armesünderblum'*, and wrote 'After Heine', but crossed both out.

67. *LP XXXII.* Written after 1910.

68. *LP XXXIII.* Written August 1900.

69. *LP XXXIV.* Written about 1905; first printed in 1914 in *The Cambridge Review*.

The mood is ironical; as the last stanza shows, May recurs, but not the same men.

70. *LP XXXV*. Written before 1910. Apparently modelled on an anonymous Greek epigram, which Housman would have met in English in *Sabrinae Corolla*, a collection he read at school when he was 17, which he said 'first turned his mind to classical studies, and gave him a genuine liking for Latin and Greek'.

71. *LP XXXVI*. The first stanza was written in 1922, the others earlier.

This is the most splendid of the astronomical poems, so long as we understand that it is not about astronomy, and that the title, as so often with Housman, is ironical or twisted. In 1926 he agreed to a request from the headmaster of Winchester for permission to print the poem in an anthology for members of the school, and said 'and if he wants a title, he can call it *Revolution*, which may be of use, as most readers do not seem to see that it is a parable'. Housman was not in the habit of explaining himself: but presumably the 'parable' is that trouble (*darkness*) shifts, but is eternal, and returns. At the height of noon, its return has already begun from the subterranean dark.

Day's beamy banner (l. 2): one of the greatest Latinists that Europe has produced seems not to have disdained to lift a phrase from the translation of Lucretius by Munro (whom Housman greatly admired). Lucretius has *radiatum insigne diei*, of which the literal translation is 'the radiant ensign or banner of day'. Munro's translation is 'ere the beamy badge of day arrive'.

. The picture of the *moon-eclipsing cone of night* (l. 7) may owe something to Lucretius's description of the earth cutting off the sun's light from the moon: 'why should the earth be able . . . to rob the moon of light, and herself on high to keep the sun hidden beneath, while the moon in her monthly journey glides through the sharp-drawn shadows of the cone'—menstrua dum rigidas coni perlabitur umbras? (*De Rerum Natura*, V, 562–4; translated by Cyril Bailey.) On the other hand, it is perhaps not necessary to have a classical precedent for the idea of the cone of darkness cast by the interposition of the earth between the sun and the moon.

If, however, the phrase is Lucretian, the conceit of *foolscap* (line 8) is Housman's. The conjunction of a dunce's cap with immensity is peculiar but impressive.

72. *LP XXXVII*. This first appeared in *The Times* of 31 October 1917 on the third anniversary of the first battle of Ypres.

Its sombre and bitter irony was not immediately understood, nor, apparently, is it always today in all quarters; at least, its irony may have been perceived, but not always its object or objects. These are God, the nature of things, and, perhaps, superior people. Housman may have had in mind the alleged remark of the German Emperor Wilhelm II, about the 'contemptible little Army' of the British at the beginning of the war. (Actually he appears to have said 'the contemptibly little Army', but the other version makes better propaganda.) The professional (mercenary) Army of Britain in 1914 was very small.

The poem has been compared with Simonides's famous epigram on the Spartans who fell at Thermopylae, which runs:

Go, tell the Spartans, thou who passest by,
That here obedient to their laws we lie.
                    (translated Mackail)

Here, if it is present at all, the irony is faint.

Line 5 is pointed in the circumstances: it is a reference to Hercules holding up the sky, while Atlas, its proper supporter, went off to get the golden Apples of the Hesperides for him.

Lucretius uses *summa rerum*, 'the sum of things', frequently, but the phrase was in English before Housman.

73. *LP XXXIX*. Written between 1920 and 1922.

74. *LP XL*. Written in April 1922 especially for *Last Poems*. In the opinion of many, including me, the loveliest of his lyrics.

It seems to me to owe something to De La Mare's beautiful poem *Farewell* (particularly to the middle stanza), which was published in *Motley and Other Poems* in 1918. We know Housman knew the poem (see Extracts from Housman's Prose Writings, 2(b)).

75. *LP XLI*. The date is unknown. According to Housman himself, the poem is indebted to Bishop Corbet's *The Fairies Farewell* of 1647, which begins 'Farewell, rewards and fairies', a jolly mock-serious lament for the old days, when fairies were about. They must, he says, have been Roman Catholics, for when Elizabeth came in, followed by James, they disappeared. Some lines are like Housman's—

> When Tom came home from labour
>   Or Ciss to milking rose
> Then merrily went their tabor
> And nimbly went their toes—

but the tone could scarcely be more different. What is fun to Corbet is sad to Housman. The eight-line stanza and the rhyme-scheme is the same, though they sound different. There is no sombre hint as there is in Housman; and I should be inclined to see more of the *tone* of the poem in Horace's *Solvitur acris hiems*—'Winter's grim chain is loosening'—(*Odes*, I, iv).

The title, *Fancy's Knell*, is taken from the song in *The Merchant of Venice*, 'Tell me where is Fancy bred'. In the song, Fancy is the love engendered by looking, and has no stable existence. This is the connection between the song and Housman's poem.

More Poems *were not selected by Housman, and were left to his brother's discretion for publication. There are many more Biblical settings and stories in MP than in the collections made by Housman himself.*

76. *MP I.* We do not know the date of this. There are only two poems on Jesus in Housman; both are sympathetic, but unbelieving.

St John, 19.41–2: 'Now in the place where he was crucified was a garden; and in the garden was a new sepulchre, wherein was never man yet laid. There laid they Jesus therefore.'

St Matthew, 28.2: 'And behold there was a great earthquake: for the angel of the Lord descended from heaven, and came and rolled back the stone from the door.'

The other poem on Jesus is No. 34.

77. *MP II.* This occurs in Housman's first poetry notebook, dating from about 1887.

Stanza 3: 'I became a deist at 13, and was an atheist at 21', Housman told a correspondent.

Stanza 1: *Exodus*, 13.21: 'And the Lord went before them by day in a pillar of a cloud to lead them the way; and by night in a pillar of fire, to give them light.' Stanza 3: *Exodus*, 14.16: 'But lift thou up thy rod, and stretch out thine hand over the sea, and divide it; and the children of Israel shall go on dry land through the midst of the sea.'

Lines 19–20 show Housman's emotional desire to believe, and also his intellectual refusal.

78. *MP III.* Of unknown date.

The first stanza of the poem seems to have Gibbon's *Decline and Fall of the Roman Empire*, Chapter II, in mind. There Gibbon speaks of the luxury of the Roman Empire:

—'The objects of oriental traffic were splendid and trifling ... precious stones, among which the pearl claimed the first rank after the diamond.' But the reference could be to any great and splendid nation of the past.

The nations of the nadir (l. 3): those of the Southern hemisphere.

79. *MP IV.* According to Laurence, the first draft of this belongs to 1890. It was first published in April 1916 in *The*

Edwardian, the magazine of King Edward's School at Bath, where his brother-in-law was headmaster.

It can scarcely be regarded as encouraging fare for youth. It seems to be an answer to a poem of Bridges, published in 1890 in *Shorter Poems*—'O youth whose hope is high'. Housman reverses the sense of Bridges's poem generally, but modifies the reversal in the last stanza to give a modest hope.

80. *MP V.* First printed in *The Quarto*, a journal of the fine arts, in 1897. It must be one of the finest translations of any poem into English ever made. Housman was deeply moved by the poem. One of his former students at Cambridge tells us how he (Housman) did something unprecedented in one of his lectures. He had completed his exposition of the text, and then, to the surprise of his audience, said, 'I should like to spend the last few minutes considering this ode simply as poetry.' Then he read the poem 'aloud with deep emotion, first in Latin, and then in an English translation of his own'. Then he added in quick, choked accents, 'That I regard as the most beautiful poem in ancient literature'; and gathering up his books and papers, he stepped hastily from the room. (Related in *Housman, 1897–1936*, Grant Richards.) It was Housman's foible to disclaim any powers as a literary critic, though he clearly had them.

Tullus, Ancus (l. 15): the third and fourth Kings of Rome. Ancus is a stock example of goodness, and is so given in Lucretius.

Aeneas (l. 16): the fabled founder of Rome, noted for his

goodness, and hence given the fixed epithet of 'pius' by Virgil.

Torquatus (l. 17): an orator, to whom the poem is addressed.

Lines 21, 22. Souls on their arrival in the Underworld appeared before a tribunal which judged their lives in the world. *equal*: 'impartial', 'just', 'fair', the sense of Latin *aequus*, now obsolete in English.

Hippolytus (l. 25) was a votary of Diana, and noted for his chastity.

Pirithōus (l. 27) was the faithful friend of Theseus, king and hero of Athens. They went together to the Underworld, perhaps to abduct Persephone. Theseus escaped, or was rescued by Hercules, but could not release his friend.

81. *MP VI*. Written about 1922. Ricks notes the contrast between the blithe movement of the verse and the dourness of the sentiment.

82. *MP IX*. See Introduction, pp. 12–13.

83. *MP X*. Written in February 1893. It was not selected by Housman for *ASL* or *LP*. It is an imitation of Sappho:

> The Moon and Pleiades have set,
>   Midnight is nigh;
> The time is passing, passing, yet
>   Alone I lie.   (trs. C. R. Haines.)

The same fragment is imitated in **MP XI*.

84. *MP XII*. There may be an echo of Milton, *Paradise Lost*,
VI, 869–70—a passage we know Housman to have
known at school—in the last two grand lines.
Eternal, foundation and *despair* are key words in Housman.

85. *MP XIII*. The *kind and foolish comrade* is the body; see No.
33, and Gow's memoir (p.249).

86. *MP XIV*. Parts of this are probably early.

87. *MP XV*.
   Hero was a beautiful priestess of Aphrodite at Sestos on
the European shore of the Hellespont. She was loved by
Leander, a young man of Abydos on the opposite shore
(i.e. Asia). Leander was accustomed to swim the channel
to Hero, who guided him by means of a lighted torch.
One stormy night, Leander was drowned, and Hero in
despair threw herself into the sea.
   The *delight* of the meeting is celebrated most sensuously
by Marlowe in his *Hero and Leander*.

88. *MP XVI*. A charming poem of wry humour and playfulness, where the remorse for unfulfilled intentions is seen in terms of opening and closing day.
Perhaps the last line owes something to Shakespeare's *Henry IV*, Part II, 4.1—

> The gaudy, blabbing and remorseful day
> Is crept into the bosom of the sea.

89. *MP XXII*. In this poem, Housman notably distorts
Biblical phrases.

cf. *Isaiah*, 55.1: 'Ho! everyone that thirsteth, come ye to the waters . . . without money and without price.'

cf. *Revelation*, 22.17: 'Let him that is athirst, come; and whosoever will, let him take the water of life freely.'

The waters are neither free nor pure in Housman. The *stolen waters* (l. 5) are those of *Proverbs* 9.17—the waters of sinful pleasure which a harlot invites the traveller to.

90. *MP XXIII*. This is the last poem of Housman's last notebook.

It is a classically pagan poem, but it has reminiscences of *Job* 3.18–22: in the grave 'the servant is free from his master'.

Charon was the official ferryman of the Underworld, in Greek mythology, who ferried the shades of the dead over the river. He was a churlish character. Unless the shade presented him with a fee, he would drive him away, and leave him to wander the deserted shore without refuge. For this reason, the Greeks were careful to put a small coin (an obolus) under the tongues of the dead as passage money.

Those who drank the waters of Lethe forgot their life in the world.

wharf (l.3) may mean merely 'bank'.

the just city (l. 7): the Underworld was regarded as a place of justice, where each received exactly what he deserved.

91. *MP XXVI*. An ingenious expression of the idea of the world existing only as it is perceived: when the observer ceases to observe, the world ceases to exist. Housman is playing with the notion of philosophical

idealism, such as is found, for instance, in the system of Bishop Berkeley.

92. *MP XXXIII*. Perhaps Housman's finest expression of the expectations and frustrations of youth. As evening is wrecked in Wales, so are those eagernesses in life.

93. *MP XXXIV*. This poem is perhaps more personal than Housman himself would have allowed to appear. Stanza 4 may refer to the spring of 1891.

94. *MP XXXVI*. See **AP XII*. There are many similar epitaphs in the Greek Anthology where young men address the passer-by. 'The resentment in the last line is absent from most Greek epitaphs.'(Marlow.)

95. *MP XXXVIII*. See Housman's translation of Sophocles on pp. 181–2.

96. *MP XLIII*.
There may be a reminiscence of Lucretius here, *De Rerum Natura*, V.91 ff., where Lucretius, speaking to Memmius, tells how the seas, and lands and sky shall in one day be hurled to ruin, 'and the massive form and fabric of the world, held up for many years, shall fall headlong' (trs. C. Bailey).

97. *MP XLV*.
'If Housman's philosophy was sound, then the great ambition of his life was unattainable and its pursuits futile; and among all his poems there are few more perfect; none of profounder melancholy, than that in which this truth is recognised.' (A. S. F. Gow on this poem in *A. E. Housman: A Sketch*.)

98. *MP XLVII.* Written in January 1925.

Housman intended it to be sung to the tune of *Brief life is here our portion*. It was so sung at the funeral ceremony in Trinity College Chapel on 4 May 1936. The melody was by Melchior, harmonised by J. S. Bach. He wrote after the last stanza: 'And then, unless forcibly restrained, the choir will sing' the Gloria.

The poem uses some of the phraseology of traditional Christian hymns: *mansion, thy children, all thy hand has made* and so on. But it represents accurately enough Housman's religious position, unless we say that even the vague *thou* who is addressed is more than he could subscribe to. As Laurence says of the hymn, it expresses 'the belief that life has no conscious hereafter'.

Laurence also says: 'He conformed . . . in the outward observances of religion, approving of the Church of England as an institution, while having no faith in its tenets.'

99. *MP XLVIII.* This was published in an Oxford poetry magazine, *Waifs and Strays*, in 1881, and was therefore written while he was an undergraduate. Its original title was *Alta Quies*: 'Deep Sleep', a phrase used by Virgil. The title here, *Parta Quies*, means 'Peace attained'.

The first three lines are on a tablet to his memory on the north wall of Ludlow Parish Church. (See *A Biographical Sketch*.)

100. *AP XVII.* First published in Laurence Housman's *Memoir* in 1937.

Translation

This is one of three translations, all choruses from Greek tragedies, first published in A. W. Pollard's anthology, *Odes from the Greek Dramatists* (1890). They express views of life congenial to Housman's own, and were no doubt chosen for that reason. Their style and metre are after the manner of Swinburne, whom the young Housman admired, in *Atalanta in Calydon*.

The other two translations are from Aeschylus (*Septem Contra Thebas*), who was Housman's favourite Greek dramatist, and Euripides (*Alcestis*).

In the last four lines, Housman has brilliantly kept the anaphora of his original. Cf. the translation by E. F. Watling in *Sophocles: The Theban Plays* (Penguin Classics):

> Of all the billows of adversity
> That break upon his head from every side
> Unceasing—from the setting sun,
> From day spring, from the blaze of noon,
> And from the pole of night.

(a) Housman as Parodist

Fragment of a Greek Tragedy

Alcmeon. Chorus

CHO. O suitably-attired-in-leather-boots
    Head of a traveller, wherefore seeking whom
    Whence by what way how purposed art thou come
    To this well-nightingaled vicinity?
    My object in enquiring is to know.
    But if you happen to be deaf and dumb
    And do not understand a word I say,
    Then wave your hand, to signify as much.
ALC. I journeyed hither a Bœotian road.
CHO. Sailing on horseback, or with feet for oars?
ALC. Plying with speed my partnership of legs.
CHO. Beneath a shining or a rainy Zeus?
ALC. Mud's sister, not himself, adorns my shoes.
CHO. To learn your name would not displease me much.
ALC. Not all that men desire do they obtain.
CHO. Might I then hear at what your presence shoots?
ALC. A shepherd's questioned mouth informed me that—
CHO. What? for I know not yet what you will say—
ALC. Nor will you ever, if you interrupt.
CHO. Proceed, and I will hold my speechless tongue.
ALC. —This house was Eriphyla's, no one's else.
CHO. Nor did he shame his throat with hateful lies.

ALC. May I then enter, passing through the door?
CHO. Go, chase into the house a lucky foot.
    And, O my son, be, on the one hand, good,
    And do not, on the other hand, be bad;
    For that is very much the safest plan.
ALC. I go into the house with heels and speed.

Chorus

In speculation   *Strophe*
I would not willingly acquire a name
    For ill-digested thought;
    But after pondering much
To this conclusion I at last have come:
    Life is uncertain.
    This truth I have written deep
    In my reflective midriff
    On tablets not of wax,
Nor with a pen did I inscribe it there,
For many reasons: *Life, I say, is not*
    A stranger to uncertainty.
Not from the flight of omen-yelling fowls
    This fact did I discover.
Nor did the Delphic tripod bark it out,
    Nor yet Dodona.
Its native ingenuity sufficed
    My self-taught diaphragm.

Why should I mention   *Antistrophe*
The Inachean daughter, loved of Zeus?
    Her whom of old the gods,
    More provident than kind,
Provided with four hoofs, two horns, one tail,

A gift not asked for
And sent her forth to learn
The unfamiliar science
Of how to chew the cud.
She therefore, all about the Argive fields,
Went cropping pale green grass and nettle-tops,
          Nor did they disagree with her.
But yet, howe'er nutritious, such repasts
          I do not hanker after:
Never may Cypris for her seat select
          My dappled liver!
Why should I mention Io? Why indeed?
          I have no notion why.

          But now does my boding heart   *Epode*
          Unhired, unaccompanied, sing
          A strain not meet for the dance.
          Yea even the palace appears
          To my yoke of circular eyes
          (The right, nor omit I the left)
          Like a slaughterhouse, so to speak,
          Garnished with woolly deaths
          And many shipwrecks of cows.
I therefore in a Cissian strain lament;
          And to the rapid,
Loud, linen-tattering thumps upon my chest
          Resounds in concert
The battering of my unlucky head.

ERIPHYLA (*within*). O, I am smitten with a hatchet's jaw;
          And that in deed and not in word alone.
CHO. I thought I heard a sound within the house

223

    Unlike the voice of one that jumps for joy.
Eri. He splits my skull, not in a friendly way,
   One more: he purposes to kill me dead.
Cho. I would not be reputed rash, but yet
   I doubt if all be gay within the house.
Eri. O! O! another stroke! that makes the third.
   He stabs me to the heart against my wish.
Cho. It that be so, thy state of health is poor;
   But thine arithmetic is quite correct.

This fragment was first published in *The Bromsgrovian*, the magazine of Housman's old school, for June 1883.

  Housman wrote a fair amount of nonsense verse, none of it very good; this parody is the funniest thing he did. It is not only a parody of a literature he loved, but, in a sense, of his own tragic sense of life.

  It is, in the first place, making fun of the oddities of style in most Greek tragedies, and of the late nineteenth-century faithful translations of them. For instance, 'head of a traveller' can be compared with Sophocles *Antigone*, 1, 'Then wave your hand to signify as much' with Clytemnestra's words to Cassandra in Aeschylus's *Agamemnon*, 1060–1:

         but if thy sense be shut
   From these my words, let thy barbarian hand
   Fulfil by gesture the default of speech

(trs. Morshead); and 'what? for I know not yet what you will say' is close to Sophocles' *Philoctetes*, 1230–4.

  In the second place, the parody is directed against the Greek tragic convention according to which violence takes place off-stage while the chorus solemnly reflects on life and protests on-stage. In the fragment, a murder is being committed in the house behind.

The scene and the thought is common in Greek tragedy; it is the cumulative effort of the stylistic parodies in the context which makes the fragment so deliciously absurd.

(b) Housman Parodied

What, still alive at twenty-two,
    A clean upstanding chap like you?
Sure, if your throat is hard to slit,
    Slit your girl's and swing for it.

Like enough, you won't be glad,
    When they come to hang you, lad.
But bacon's not the only thing
    That's cured by hanging from a string.

When the blotting-pad of night
    Sucks the latest drop of light,
Lads whose job is still to do
    Shall whet their knives and think of you.

Nearly all parodies of Housman are bad. This one, by Hugh Kingsmill, is by far the best, as Housman himself thought.

This catches both Housman's style and thought, with its bold conceits and colloquial phrase, and its suicidal motif.

Extracts from Housman's Prose Writings

Housman was no less a master of prose than of poetry. Indeed, his prose has some of the same qualities as his poetry: incisiveness, clarity, the use from time to time of colloquial phrase, and an easy familiarity with the Bible. In particular, it would be difficult to match his power of vivid and downright invective and his flashes or sustained passages of wit. This is shown especially in the Preface to *Book I of Manilius* (1903), where he reviews the efforts of editors and commentators before him to deal with the text of Manilius. His brother Laurence has pointed out that however ruthless his treatment of intellectual foolishness and pretentious learning was, he was gentle with moral foolishness, especially that of 'troubled youth' (see *AP XVIII*—'O who is that young sinner?'). At the end of the Preface to *Book V of Manilius*, Housman lists the qualifications of a conjectural emendator and claims that he has them (Extract 2(b)). His claim is true, and affords some justification for his acerbity in treating the work of less skilled and devoted practitioners.

Housman kept an armoury of offensive weapons, which included both rapier and bludgeon, and there is no doubt he enjoyed furnishing it. His brother records that one of his notebooks has about five pages of 'stored ammunition', some with names attached, some without. The following is a specimen:

'I do not know upon what subject —— will next employ his versatile incapacity. He is very well—dangerously well.'

Laurence speaks of the 'jolly ferocity' with which he attacks the dunces in his own field of textual criticism. Not all would agree with 'jolly', though the word suggests the relish with which the insolence seems launched. Housman regarded himself as a soldier in the world of scholarship, striving with fellow-soldiers 'to achieve the common end of all, to set back the frontiers of darkness'. It is for this reason that he is so lavish with his contempt for pretension, muddle-headedness, and intellectual slackness. He is equally lavish with his praise, where he thought it deserved, as he thought Bentley deserved it (Extract 2(a)).

1 From the *Introductory Lecture* (1892)
(In October 1892, Housman was about to enter on his duties as Professor of Latin at University College, London. This is his first lecture, which is fundamentally concerned with learning for its own sake, and its detachment from merely utilitarian considerations, as they were expressed by Herbert Spencer. Housman said later it was not wholly sincere; if this means that he exaggerated his point, this is true; but he believed heart and soul in the point.)

1 (a) 'The partisans of Science define the aim of learning to be utility. I do not mean to say that any eminent man of science commits himself to this opinion: some of them have publicly and scornfully repudiated it, and all of them, I imagine, reject it in their hearts. But there is no denying that this is the view which makes Science popular; this is

the impression under which the British merchant or manufacturer dies and leaves his money to endow scientific education. And since this impression, though false, is nevertheless beneficent in its results, those who are interested in scientific pursuits may very well consider that it is no business of theirs to dispel a delusion which promises so well for the world in general and for themselves in particular. The popular view, I say, is that the aim of acquiring knowledge is to equip one's self for the business of life; that accordingly the knowledge most to be sought after is the knowledge which equips one best; and that this knowledge is Science. And the popular view has the very distinguished countenance of Mr Herbert Spencer. Mr Spencer, in his well-known treatise on Education, pronounces that education to be of most value which prepares us for self-preservation by preparing us for securing the necessaries of life; and that is education in the sciences. "For," says he, "leaving out only some very small classes, what are all men employed in? They are employed in the production, preparation and distribution of commodities. And on what does efficiency in the production, preparation and distribution of commodities depend? It depends on the use of methods fitted to the respective natures of these commodities; it depends on an adequate acquaintance with their physical, chemical and vital properties, as the case may be; that is, it depends on Science." And then he proceeds with his usual exactness of detail to shew in what way each several science serves to render one efficient in producing, preparing or distributing commodities.

Now to begin with, it is evident that if we are to pursue Science simply in order to obtain an adequate acquaintance with the physical, chemical and vital properties of the commodities which we produce, prepare or distribute, we shall not need to pursue Science far. Mr Spencer duly rehearses the list of the sciences, and is at much pains to demonstrate the bearing of each science on the arts of life. Take one for a specimen. I suppose that in no science have Englishmen more distinguished themselves than in astronomy: one need but mention the name of Isaac Newton. And it is a science which has not only fascinated the profoundest intellects but has always laid a strong hold on the popular imagination, so that, for example, our newspapers found it paid them to fill a good deal of space with articles about the present apposition of the planet Mars. And now listen to the reasons why we are to study astronomy. "Of the concrete sciences we come first to Astronomy. Out of this has grown that art of navigation which has made possible the enormous foreign commerce that supports a large part of our population, while supplying us with many necessaries and most of our luxuries." That is all there is to say about astronomy: that navigation has grown out of it. Well then, we want no Isaac Newtons; let them carry their *Principias* to another market. Astronomy is a squeezed orange as far as we are concerned. Astronomers may transfer their residence to the remotest world they can discover, and welcome, for all the need we have of them here: the enormous foreign commerce which Mr Spencer speaks of will still enable this island to be overpopulated, and our currants and cocoanuts will continue to arrive with their former regularity. Hundreds and hundreds of years ago astronomy had reached the point which satisfies our modest requirements: it had given birth to navigation. They were conversing in Athens four centuries before Christ, and a young Spencerian named Glaucon already found more than this to say in praise of the utility of astronomy. "Shall we make astronomy one of our studies," asked Socrates, "or do you dissent?" "No, I agree," said Glaucon, "for to have an intimate acquaintance with seasons, and months, and years, is an advantage not only to the farmer and the navigator, but also, in an equal degree, to the general"—an aspect of astronomical science which appears to have escaped Mr Spencer's notice.

Astronomy, you may say, is not a fair example to take, because of all sciences it is perhaps the one which least concerns the arts of life. May be; but this difference between astronomy and other sciences is a difference of degree alone. Just as even astronomy, though it touches practical life but little, does nevertheless touch it, so those sciences, such as chemistry and physics, which are the most intimately and widely concerned with practical life, nevertheless throughout a great portion of their range have no contact with it at all. If it is in order to secure the necessaries of life that we are to study chemistry and physics, we shall study them further no doubt than we shall for that reason study astronomy, but not so far by a long way as chemists and physicists do in fact study them now. Electric lighting and aniline dyes and other such magnificent alleviations of human destiny do not spring into being at every forward step in our knowledge of the physical forces and chemical composition of the universe: they are merely occasional incidents, flowers by the way. Much in both sciences which the chemist and the physicist study with intense interest and delight will be set aside as curious and unprofitable learning by our producer, preparer or distributor of commodities. In short, the fact is, that what man will seek to acquaint himself with in order to prepare him for securing the necessaries of life is not Science, but the indispensable minimum of Science.

And just as our knowledge of Science need not be deep, so too it need not be wide. Mr Spencer shews that every science is of some use to some man or another. But not every science is of use to every man. Geometry, he points out, is useful to the carpenter, and chemistry to the calico-printer. True; but geometry is not useful to the calico-printer, nor chemistry to the carpenter. If it is to secure the necessaries of life that men pursue Science, the sciences that each man needs to pursue are few. In addition to the initial studies of reading, writing and arithmetic, he needs to acquaint himself with those sciences, or rather, as I said before, with the indispensable minimum of those sciences, which concern the trade or the art he earns his bread by: the dyer with chemistry, the carpenter with geometry, the navigator with astronomy. But there he can stop. Mr Spencer appears to apprehend this; and since such a result is far from his desires, he attempts, in the case of one or two sciences, to shew that no one can neglect them with impunity. The following, for instance, is the method by which he endeavours to terrorise us into studying geology. We may, any of us, some day, take shares in a joint-stock company; and that company may engage in mining operations; and those operations may be directed to the discovery of coal; and for want of geological information the joint-stock company may go mining for coal under the old red sandstone, where there is no coal. and then the mining operations will be fruitless, and the joint-stock company will come to grief, and where shall we be then? This is, indeed, to eat the bread of carefulness. After all, men have been known to complete their pilgrimage through this vale of tears without taking shares in a joint-stock company. But the true reply to Mr Spencer's intimidations I imagine to be this: that the attempt to fortify man's estate against all contingencies by such precautions as these is in the first place interminable and in the second place hopeless. As Sarpedon says to Glaucus in the *Iliad*, a hundred thousand fates stand close to us always, which none can flee and none avoid. The complexity of the universe is infinite, and the days of a man's life are threescore years and ten. One lifetime, nine lifetimes are not long enough for the task of blocking every cranny through which calamity may enter. And say that we could thus triumphantly succeed in the attempt at self-preservation; say that we could thus impregnably secure the necessaries of existence; even then the true business of life is not so much as begun. Existence is not itself a good thing, that we should spend a lifetime securing its necessaries: a life spent, however victoriously, in securing the necessaries of life is no more than an elaborate furnishing and decoration of apartments for the reception of a guest who is never to come. Our business here is not to live, but to live happily. We may seem to be occupied, as Mr Spencer says, in the production, preparation and distribution of commodities; but our true occupation is to manufacture from the raw material of life the fabric of happiness; and if we are ever to set about our work we must make up our minds to risk something. Absolute security for existence is unattainable, and no wise man will pursue it; for if we must go to these lengths in the attempt at self-preservation we shall die before ever we have begun to

live. Reasonable security is attainable; but it is attainable
without any wide study of Science.'

1 (b) 'Perhaps it will be objected that we see, every day of
our lives, plenty of people who exhibit no pleasure in
learning and experience no desire to know; people, as
Plato agreeably puts it, who wallow in ignorance with the
complacency of a brutal hog. We do; and here is the
reason. If the cravings of hunger and thirst are denied
satisfaction, if a man is kept from food and drink, the man
starves to death, and there is an end of him. This is a result
which arrests the attention of even the least observant
mind; so it is generally recognised that hunger and thirst
cannot be neglected with impunity, that a man ought to
eat and drink. But if the craving for knowledge is denied
satisfaction, the result which follows is not so striking to
the eye. The man, worse luck, does not starve to death.
He still preserves the aspect and motions of a living human
being; so people think that the hunger and thirst for
knowledge can be neglected with impunity. And yet,
though the man does not die altogether, part of him dies,
part of him starves to death: as Plato says, he never attains
completeness and health, but walks lame to the end of his
life and returns imperfect and good for nothing to the
world below.

But the desire of knowledge, stifle it though you may, is
none the less originally born with every man; and nature
does not implant desires in us for nothing, nor endow us
with faculties in vain. "Sure," says Hamlet,

"Sure, He that made us with such large discourse,
Looking before and after, gave us not
That capability and godlike reason
To fust in us unused."

The faculty of learning is ours that we may find in its
exercise that delight which arises from the unimpeded
activity of any energy in the groove nature meant it to run
in. Let a man acquire knowledge not for this or that
external and incidental good which may chance to result
from it, but for itself; not because it is useful or ornamen-
tal, but because it is knowledge, and therefore good for
man to acquire. "Brothers," says Ulysses in Dante, when
with his old and tardy companions he had left Seville on
the right hand and Ceuta on the other, and was come to
that narrow pass where Hercules assigned his landmarks
to hinder man from venturing farther: "Brothers, who
through a hundred thousand dangers have reached the
West, deny not, to this brief vigil of your senses that re-
mains, experience of the unpeopled world behind the
sunset. Consider of what seed ye are sprung: ye were not
formed to live like brutes, but to follow virtue and know-
ledge." For knowledge resembles virtue in this, and differs
in this from other possessions, that it is not merely a
means of procuring good, but is good in itself simply: it is
not a coin which we pay down to purchase happiness, but
has happiness indissolubly bound up with it. Fortitude and
continence and honesty are not commended to us on the
ground that they conduce, as on the whole they do con-
duce, to material success, nor yet on the ground that they
will be rewarded hereafter: those whose office it is to ex-
hort mankind to virtue are ashamed to degrade the cause

they plead by proffering such lures as these. And let us too disdain to take lower ground in commending knowledge: let us insist that the pursuit of knowledge, like the pursuit of righteousness, is part of man's duty to himself; and remember the Scripture where it is written: "He that refuseth instruction despiseth his own soul."

I will not say, as Prof. Tyndall has somewhere said, that all happiness belongs to him who can say from his heart "I covet truth". Entire happiness is not attainable either by this or by any other method. Nay it may be urged on the contrary that the pursuit of truth in some directions is even injurious to happiness, because it compels us to take leave of delusions which were pleasant while they lasted. It may be urged that the light shed on the origin and destiny of man by the pursuit of truth in some directions is not altogether a cheerful light. It may be urged that man stands today in the position of one who has been reared from his cradle as the child of a noble race and the heir to great possessions, and who finds at his coming of age that he has been deceived alike as to his origin and his expectations; that he neither springs of the high lineage he fancied, nor will inherit the vast estate he looked for, but must put off his towering pride, and contract his boundless hopes, and begin the world anew from a lower level: and this, it may be urged, comes of pursuing knowledge. But even conceding this, I suppose the answer to be that knowledge, and especially disagreeable knowledge, cannot by any art be totally excluded even from those who do not seek it. Wisdom, said Aeschylus long ago, comes to men whether they will or no. The house of delusions is cheap to build, but draughty to live in, and ready at any instant to fall; and it is surely truer prudence to move our furniture betimes into the open air than to stay indoors until our tenement tumbles about our ears. It is and it must in the long run be better for a man to see things as they are than to be ignorant of them; just as there is less fear of stumbling or of striking against corners in the daylight than in the dark.

Nor again will I pretend that, as Bacon asserts, "the pleasure and delight of knowledge and learning far surpasseth all other in nature". This is too much the language of a salesman crying his own wares. The pleasures of the intellect are notoriously less vivid than either the pleasures of sense or the pleasures of the affections; and therefore, especially in the season of youth, the pursuit of knowledge is likely enough to be neglected and lightly esteemed in comparison with other pursuits offering much stronger immediate attractions. But the pleasure of learning and knowing, though not the keenest, is yet the least perishable of pleasures; the least subject to external things, and the play of chance, and the wear of time. And as a prudent man puts money by to serve as a provision for the material wants of his old age, so too he needs to lay up against the end of his days provision for the intellect. As the years go by, comparative values are found to alter: Time, says Sophocles, takes many things which once were pleasures and brings them nearer to pain. In the day when the strong men shall bow themselves, and desire shall fail, it will be a matter of yet more concern than now, whether one can say "my mind to me a kingdom is"; and whether the windows of the soul look out upon a broad and delightful landscape, or face nothing but a brick wall.

Well then, once we have recognised that knowledge in itself is good for man, we shall need to invent no pretexts for studying this subject or that; we shall import no extraneous considerations of use or ornament to justify us in learning one thing rather than another. If a certain department of knowledge specially attracts a man, let him study that, and study it because it attracts him; and let him not fabricate excuses for that which requires no excuse, but rest assured that the reason why it most attracts him is that it is best for him. The majority of mankind, as is only natural, will be most attracted by those sciences which most nearly concern human life; those sciences which, in Bacon's phrase, are drenched in flesh and blood, or, in the more elegant language of the *Daily Telegraph*, palpitate with actuality. The men who are attracted to the drier and the less palpitating sciences, say logic or pure mathematics or textual criticism, are likely to be fewer in number; but they are not to suppose that the comparative unpopularity of such learning renders it any the less worthy of pursuit. Nay they may if they like console themselves with Bacon's observation that "this same *lumen siccum* doth parch and offend most men's watery and soft natures", and infer, if it pleases them, that their natures are less soft and watery than other men's. But be that as it may, we can all dwell together in unity without crying up our own pursuits or depreciating the pursuits of others on factitious grounds. We are not like the Ottoman sultans of old time, who thought they could never enjoy a moment's security till they had murdered all their brothers. There is no rivalry between the studies of Arts and Laws and Science but the rivalry of fellow-soldiers in striving which can most victoriously achieve the common end of all, to set back the frontier of darkness.'

2. Extracts from the Prefaces

2 (a) From the Preface to *Book I of Manilius*

'Great as was Scaliger's achievement it is yet surpassed and far surpassed by Bentley's: Scaliger at the side of Bentley is no more than a marvellous boy. In mere quantity indeed the corrections of the critic who came first may be the more imposing, but it is significant that Scaliger accomplished most in the easiest parts of the poem and Bentley in the hardest. The firm strength and piercing edge and arrowy swiftness of his intellect, his matchless facility and adroitness and resource, were never so triumphant as where defeat seemed sure; and yet it is other virtues that one most admires and welcomes as one turns from the smoky fire of Scaliger's genius to the sky and air of Bentley's: his lucidity, his sanity, his just and simple and straightforward fashion of thought.'

'If a man will comprehend the richness and variety of the universe, and inspire his mind with a due measure of wonder and of awe, he must contemplate the human intellect not only on its heights of genius but in its abysses of ineptitude; and it might be fruitlessly debated to the end of time whether Richard Bentley or Elias Stoeber was the more marvellous work of the Creator: Elias Stoeber, whose reprint of Bentley's text, with a commentary intended to confute it, saw the light in 1767 at Strasburg, a city still famous for its geese. This commentary is a performance in comparison with which the *Aetna* of Mr S. Sudhaus is a work of science and of genius. Stoeber's mind, though that is no name to call it by, was one which turned as unswervingly to the false, the meaningless, the unmetrical, and the ungrammatical, as the needle to the pole.'

'They say [of Friedrich Jacob, an early nineteenth-century editor of Manilius] that he was born of human parentage; but if so he must have been suckled by Caucasian tigers. . . . Not only had Jacob no sense for grammar, no sense for coherency, no sense for sense, but being himself possessed by a passion for the clumsy and the hispid, he imputed this disgusting taste to all the authors whom he edited; and Manilius, the one Latin poet who excels even Ovid in verbal point and smartness, is accordingly constrained to write the sort of poetry which might have been composed by Nebuchadnezzar when he was driven from men and did eat grass as oxen.'

'But the worst of having no judgment is that one never misses it, and buoyantly embarks without it upon enterprises in which it is not so much a convenience as a necessity.'

'For assuredly there is no trade on earth, excepting textual criticism, in which the name of prudence would be given to that habit of mind which in ordinary human life is called credulity.

The average man, if he meddles with criticism at all, is a conservative critic. His opinions are determined not by his reason,—"the bulk of mankind" says Swift "is as well qualified for flying as for thinking,"—but by his passions; and the faintest of all human passions is the love of truth. He believes that the text of ancient authors is generally sound, not because he has acquainted himself with the elements of the problem, but because he would feel uncomfortable if he did not believe it; just as he believes, on

the same cogent evidence, that he is a fine fellow, and that
he will rise again from the dead.'

2 (b) From the Preface to *Book V of Manilius* (1930)
'The corrections of Ellis were rather more numerous, and
one or two of them were very pretty, but his readers were
in perpetual contact with the intellect of an idiot child.'

'The Latin commentary was separately published in 1921
with no small magnificence by the royal academy of
sciences at Amsterdam. What it most resembles is a mag-
pie's nest. With the rarest exceptions, all that it contains
of any value, whether interpretation or illustration, is
taken from others, and usually without acknowledgment.'

'It surprises me that so many people should feel them-
selves qualified to weigh conjectures in their balance and
to pronounce them good or bad, probable or improbable.
Judging an emendation requires in some measure the
same qualities as emendation itself, and the requirement
is formidable. To read attentively, think correctly, omit
no relevant consideration, and repress self-will, are not
ordinary accomplishments; yet an emendator needs much
besides: just literary perception, congenial intimacy with
the author, experience which must have been won by
study, and mother wit which he must have brought from
his mother's womb.
It may be asked whether I think that I myself possess this
outfit, or even most of it; and if I answer yes, that will be
a new example of my notorious arrogance. I had rather be
arrogant than impudent. I should not have undertaken to
edit Manilius unless I had believed that I was fit for the

task; and in particular I think myself a better judge of emendation, both when to emend and how to emend, than most others.

The following stanza of Mr de la Mare's "Fare Well" first met my eyes, thus printed, in a newspaper review.

> Oh, when this my dust surrenders
> Hand, foot, lip, to dust again,
> May these loved and loving faces
>   Please other men!
>
> May the rustling harvest hedgerow
> Still the Traveller's Joy entwine,
> And as happy children gather
>   Posies once mine.

I knew in a moment that Mr de la Mare had not written *rustling*, and in another moment I had found the true word. But if the book of poems had perished and the verse survived only in the review, who would have believed me rather than the compositor? The bulk of the reading public would have been perfectly content with *rustling*, nay they would sincerely have preferred it to the epithet which the poet chose. If I had been so ill-advised as to publish my emendation, I should have been told that *rustling* was exquisitely apt and poetical, because hedgerows do rustle, especially in autumn, when the leaves are dry, and when straws and ears from the passing harvest-wain (to which "harvest" is so plain an allusion that only a pedant like me could miss it) are hanging caught in the twigs; and I should have been recommended to quit my dusty (or musty) books and make a belated acquaintance with the sights and sounds of the English countryside.'

3. From *The Name and Nature of Poetry*
(This was given as the Leslie Stephen Lecture for 1933 in Cambridge. Housman, both here and in the *Introductory Lecture*, had spoken of the faculty of literary criticism as the rarest of Heaven's gifts, and had disclaimed any power in this art for himself. He later confessed, under pressure, to Hardy, the mathematician, that he had perhaps exaggerated the importance of the good literary critic in apparently making him rarer than the creative artist.

3 (a) 'When I examine my mind and try to discern clearly in the matter, I cannot satisfy myself that there are any such things as poetical ideas. No truth, it seems to me, is too precious, no observation too profound, and no sentiment too exalted to be expressed in prose. The utmost that I could admit is that some ideas do, while others do not, lend themselves kindly to poetical expression; and that these receive from poetry an enhancement which glorifies and almost transfigures them, and which is not perceived to be a separate thing except by analysis.

"Whosoever will save his life shall lose it, and whosoever will lose his life shall find it." That is the most important truth which has ever been uttered, and the greatest discovery ever made in the moral world; but I do not find in it anything which I should call poetical. On the other hand, when Wisdom says in the Proverbs "He that sinneth against me wrongeth his own soul; all they that hate me, love death", that is to me poetry, because of the words in which the idea is clothed; and as for the seventh verse of the forty-ninth Psalm in the Book of Common Prayer, "But no man may deliver his brother, nor make agreement unto God for him", that is to me poetry so moving that I can hardly keep my voice steady in reading it. And that this is the effect of language I can ascertain by experiment: the same thought in the Bible version, "None of them can by any means redeem his brother, nor give to God a ransom for him", I can read without emotion.

Poetry is not the thing said but a way of saying it. Can it then be isolated and studied by itself? for the combination of language with its intellectual content, its meaning, is as close a union as can well be imagined. Is there such a thing as pure unmingled poetry, poetry independent of meaning?

Even when poetry has a meaning, as it usually has, it may be inadvisable to draw it out. "Poetry gives most pleasure" said Coleridge "when only generally and not perfectly understood"; and perfect understanding will sometimes almost extinguish pleasure. *The Haunted Palace* is one of Poe's best poems so long as we are content to swim in the sensations it evokes and only vaguely to apprehend the allegory. We are roused to discomfort, at least I am, when we begin to perceive how exact in detail the allegory is; when it dawns upon us that the fair palace door is Roderick Usher's mouth, the pearl and ruby his teeth and lips, the yellow banners his hair, the ramparts plumed and pallid his forehead, and when we are reduced to hoping, for it is no more than a hope, that the winged odours have no connexion with hair-oil.

Meaning is of the intellect, poetry is not. If it were, the eighteenth century would have been able to write it better. As matters actually stand, who are the English poets of that age in whom pre-eminently one can hear and recognise the true poetic accent emerging clearly from the contemporary dialect? These four: Collins, Christopher

Smart, Cowper, and Blake. And what other characteristic had these four in common? They were mad. Remember Plato: "He who without the Muses' madness in his soul comes knocking at the door of poesy and thinks that art will make him anything fit to be called a poet, finds that the poetry which he indites in his sober senses is beaten hollow by the poetry of madmen."

That the intellect is not the fount of poetry, that it may actually hinder its production, and that it cannot even be trusted to recognise poetry when produced, is best seen in the case of Smart. Neither the prize founded in this University by the Rev. Thomas Seaton nor the successive contemplation of five several attributes of the Supreme Being could incite him to good poetry while he was sane. The only poem by which he is remembered, a poem which came to its own in the kinder climate of the nineteenth century and has inspired one of the best poems of the twentieth, was written, if not, as tradition says, in actual confinement, at any rate very soon after release; and when the eighteenth century, the age of sanity and intelligence, collected his poetical works, it excluded this piece as "bearing melancholy proofs of the recent estrangement of his mind".

Collins and Cowper, though they saw the inside of mad-houses, are not supposed to have written any of their poetry there; and Blake was never mad enough to be locked up. But elements of their nature were more or less insurgent against the centralised tyranny of the intellect, and their brains were not thrones on which the great usurper could sit secure. And so it strangely came to pass that in the eighteenth century, the age of prose and of unsound or unsatisfying poetry, there sprang up one well of the purest inspiration. For me the most poetical of all poets is Blake. I find his lyrical note as beautiful as Shakespeare's and more beautiful than anyone else's; and I call him more poetical than Shakespeare, even though Shakespeare has so much more poetry, because poetry in him preponderates more than in Shakespeare over everything else, and instead of being confounded in a great river can be drunk pure from a slender channel of its own. Shakespeare is rich in thought, and his meaning has power of itself to move us, even if the poetry were not there: Blake's meaning is often unimportant or virtually nonexistent, so that we can listen with all our hearing to his celestial tune.

Even Shakespeare, who had so much to say, would sometimes pour out his loveliest poetry in saying nothing.

> Take O take those lips away
>   That so sweetly were forsworn,
> And those eyes, the break of day,
>   Lights that do mislead the morn;
> But my kisses bring again,
>   bring again,
> Seals of love, but seal'd in vain,
>   seal'd in vain.

That is nonsense; but it is ravishing poetry. When Shakespeare fills such poetry with thought, and thought which is worthy of it, as in *Fear no more the heat o' the sun* or *O mistress mine, where are you roaming?* those songs, the very summits of lyrical achievement, are indeed greater and more moving poems, but I hardly know how to call them more poetical.'

3 (b) 'In most poets, as I said, poetry is less often found thus disengaged from its usual concomitants, from certain things with which it naturally unites itself and seems to blend indistinguishably. For instance:

> Sorrow, that is not sorrow, but delight;
> And miserable love, that is not pain
> To hear of, for the glory that redounds
> Therefrom to human kind, and what we are.

The feeling with which those lines are read is composite, for one constituent is supplied by the depth and penetrating truth of the thought. Again:

> Though love repine and reason chafe,
> There came a voice without reply,—
> " 'Tis man's perdition to be safe,
> When for the truth he ought to die".

Much of the emotion kindled by that verse can be referred to the nobility of the sentiment. But in these six simple words of Milton—

> Nymphs and shepherds, dance no more—

what is it that can draw tears, as I know it can, to the eyes of more readers than one? What in the world is there to cry about? Why have the mere words the physical effect of pathos when the sense of the passage is blithe and gay? I can only say, because they are poetry, and find their way to something in man which is obscure and latent, something older than the present organisation of his nature, like the patches of fen which still linger here and there in the drained lands of Cambridgeshire.

Poetry indeed seems to me more physical than intellectual. A year or two ago, in common with others, I received from America a request that I would define poetry. I replied that I could no more define poetry than a terrier can define a rat, but that I thought we both recognised the object by the symptoms which it provokes in us. One of these symptoms was described in connexion with another object by Eliphaz the Temanite: "A spirit passed before my face: the hair of my flesh stood up." Experience has taught me, when I am shaving of a morning, to keep watch over my thoughts, because if a line of poetry strays into my memory, my skin bristles so that the razor ceases to act. This particular symptom is accompanied by a shiver down the spine; there is another which consists in a constriction of the throat and a precipitation of water to the eyes; and there is a third which I can only describe by borrowing a phrase from one of Keats's last letters, where he says, speaking of Fanny Brawne, "everything that reminds me of her goes through me like a spear". The seat of this sensation is the pit of the stomach.'

Selected Bibliography

TEXTS

The Collected Poems of A. E. Housman (Jonathan Cape, paperback, 1967)

A. E. Housman: Selected Prose, ed. John Carter (Cambridge University Press)

BIOGRAPHY

A. E. Housman: A Sketch, A. S. F. Gow (Cambridge, 1936)
An impeccable outline by a much younger classical colleague at Trinity College, Cambridge, together with a list of his writings.

A.E.H.: Some Poems, Some Letters, and a Personal Memoir by his Brother, Laurence Housman (Cape, 1937)
This includes a complete list of dated poems.

Housman, 1897–1936, Grant Richards (London, 1941)
Richards was Housman's first publisher, and his friend until Housman died.
The book resembles what Housman called another commentary, 'a magpie's nest'. Its most valuable portion is Housman's reply to a questionnaire from a student called Maurice Pollet about his life, opinions and art (see *A Biographical Outline*, p. 37).

A Buried Life, PercyWithers (Cape, 1940)
Withers knew Housman well over his last 19 years.

A. Books

A. E. Housman, Scholar and Poet, Norman Marlow (Routledge and Kegan Paul, 1958)
Sound. Marlow is a classical scholar himself.

A. E. Housman, A Collection of Critical Essays, ed. Christopher Ricks (A Spectrum Paperback. Prentice-Hall, Inc., N.J., U.S.A., 1968)
It has some interesting points of view.

B. Articles and Essays

A. E. Housman and Music, William White (in *Music and Letters*, October 1943)
I have quoted from this in my Introduction.

Figures in Modern Literature, J. B. Priestley (John Lane, 1924; reprinted essay from *The London Mercury*)

Independent Essays, John Sparrow (Faber, 1963)
This contains two essays, one called *The Shropshire Lad at Fifty* (1946), and *Housman Obscured* (1958).

Index of First lines

Index of Titled Poems